I0640564

John Gordon

A New Estimate of Manners and Principles

Being a comparison between ancient and modern times

.

John Gordon

A New Estimate of Manners and Principles
Being a comparison between ancient and modern times

ISBN/EAN: 9783337175009

Printed in Europe, USA, Canada, Australia, Japan

Cover: Foto ©ninafisch / pixelio.de

More available books at **www.hansebooks.com**

A NEW ESTIMATE

OF

MANNERS and PRINCIPLES:

Being a COMPARISON between

Ancient and Modern TIMES,

In the three Great Articles

OF

Knowledge, Happiness, and *Virtue;*

Both with Refpect

To MANKIND at Large,

AND TO

This KINGDOM in Particular.

——————— *Demo unum, demo et item unum* ;
Dum cadat elufus ratione ruentis acervi,
Qui redit in faftos, et VIRTUTEM ÆSTIMAT ANNIS.

CAMBRIDGE,

Printed by J. BENTHAM, Printer to the UNIVERSITY ;
for W. THURLBOURN and J. WOODYER, in *Cambridge* ;
and fold by A. MILLAR in the *Strand*, R. & J. DODSLEY
in *Pall Mall*, & J. BEECROFT in *Pater-nofter Row, London.*

M.DCC.LX.

AN

A P O L O G Y

TO THE

AUTHOR of a former *Eſtimate*.

SIR,

WHEN I preſumed to call my
preſent production, *A New
Eſtimate*; I did not intend to have the
ſpurious iſſue laid at your door. Far
be the thought from me, of attempting to injure any man's fair fame, by
ſuch baſe means! beſides, the make
and features of my poor offspring are
ſo totally unlike your's, that an impoſition of that kind, had I aimed at it,
would have been too glaring to paſs un-
detected.

I will freely own to you therefore, that it was merely a Bookſeller's conſideration, which induced me to borrow the title of your late, celebrated work: I was told, that the ſale of a Book depended intirely upon the name it bore; which indeed I was inclined beforehand to think might, in a great meaſure, be the caſe; though, I own, I never, till now, apprehended it's meaning to be, what I find it is, not a metaphorical one, but ſtrictly literal; not ſignifying the reputation of a book, but merely it's title-page. And it ſeems, Bookſellers are as ſhy of ſtanding for a book, as ſome Godfathers are, in another inſtance; unleſs they can have the naming of the Brat, when they attend, with other Goſſips, on the due celebration of that rite. I hope therefore, a young Author, who would make his appearance in the world with as much advantage, as he could, may be excuſed for endeavouring to uſher in his firſt performance under a favorite name.

But

But I have more than this to plead in my defence; for I find, what I have done is no more, than what is conſtantly practiſed, and is impoſed as a kind of tax upon you great Authors; which, by cuſtom, you are obliged to ſubmit to: no ſooner comes out *High life below ſtairs*, and has, what they call, a Run; but out pops a paultry imitation, intitled, *Low life above ſtairs*. No wonder then, if, after a valuable book is publiſhed, called an *Eſtimate*, you ſhould ſee following, at a proper diſtance, a *New Eſtimate*; which perhaps, for the future, will come out, year after year, like a new year's Almanac, or a new Memorandum Book.

But however alike I may be, in other reſpects, to my brother Imitators; I cannot help claiming this ſuperiority to myſelf, that I fairly declare, how the caſe ſtands; whereas I find, this is a point, which, in general, is moſt induſtriouſly concealed: for, upon examining with the utmoſt diligence, I

cannot,

cannot, in all that numberlefs train of Magazines, with which the literary world is at prefent fo plentifully ftored, difcover one, that has paid the leaft refpect or acknowledgment to Mr. *E. Cave,* at St. *John's Gate*; though the undoubted and indifputable, original Author of the firft of thefe commodious repofitories of human learning, commonly called, *The Gentleman's Magazine.* Neither can I help obferving, in what a barefaced manner Mr. *Baldwin,* Mr. *Newbery,* Mr. *Sheepey,* and others yearly go on to publifh, what they are pleafed to call, their *Pocket Companions, Daily Journals,* &c. without once taking notice of what Meff^rs *R. & J. Dodfley* conftantly inform them of, that *Their's,* "as it was the *firft,* fo it is ftill the *beft* book of the kind."

I fhall mention but one thing more in my vindication; that I have ftayed long enough to fee, whether you would continue the work, or no. But, though you had now fo fair an opportunity, at the

the end of the glorious 1759, of tell‑ing your countrymen better things; and of fhewing the wonderful and furprif‑ing efficacy of your writings; which, in fo fhort a time, have brought about fuch an effectual alteration in the man‑ners of his Majefty's fubjects; yet I per‑ceive, you have let it flip: which inclines me to think, you have intirely given up the bufinefs of *Eftimate-making*. And therefore I look upon myfelf as fully excufed for attempting to avail myfelf of the opening, to fet up in that branch of trade; in which, if I am but fo hap‑py, as to give as much fatisfaction to thofe, who fhall honor me with their cuftom, as you did; I fhall ever efteem it one of the moft fortunate events in my whole life.

Thinking myfelf, by this time, fully juftified in your opinion for the ftep I have taken, I am emboldened to take the farther liberty of making your mo‑defty give way to my importunity, whilft I fupply what I fuppofe you

a 4   thought

thought would not come fo properly from yourfelf, and enlarge a little on the merit of your late, ineftimable *Eftimate.*

When one reads in it then the following, animated defcription of the *ruling manners* of this kingdom, which obtained only two years ago: " A man " who fhould go out of the common " road of life, in purfuit of glory, and " ferve the public at the expence of his " eafe, his fortune, or his pleafure, " would be ftared and laughed at in " every fafhionable circle, as a filly " fellow, who meddled with things that " did not concern him: as an ideot, " who preferred fhadows to realities, " and needlefs toil to pleafurable enjoy- " ment." And, that " The laurel wreath, " once afpired after as the higheft object " of ambition, would now be rated at " the market price of it's materials, and " derided as a *three-penny Crown.*" When one reads thefe, I fay, and fome other *fimilar* paffages in your book, and
hears

hears you farther declare, that " A
" change of manners, and principles
" may be juftly regarded as an impoffi-
" ble event, during the prefent age;
" and rather to be wifhed than hoped
" for in the next;" and yet perceives
at the fame time, that this change has
in fact already happened; to fuch a
degree, that they, who were then, as
you tenderly exprefs it, *the contempt of
Europe*, are now become the terror of
it: to what can one afcribe fuch an
amazing alteration? To nothing, am I
ready to anfwer, fince miracles have
ceafed, but to the writings of a certain
great author; which undoubtedly contained the grand fpecific, that has
wrought this cure: which by fome fe-
cret and infenfible kind of opera-
tion has produced fuch fudden and
furprizing effects, though the manner may be difficult to be explain-
ed; which, by diffufing at once fuch
a new and unufual fpirit through the
camp and the navy, has fo amply re-
trieved

trieved the honor of our arms, and rais-
ed to so high a pitch the reputation of
our country; which, by it's wonderful influence in rouzing the indolent,
and animating the carelefs; in giving
manliness to the effeminate; public
love to the felfifh; and courage to the
voluptuary; has thus totally changed
the whole face of our affairs: and made
the upper ranks of our fellow-fubjects
rife up in arms, as one man, with the
true *spirit of union and defence*, in fupport of *Britifh* Liberty at home; and
abroad has caufed a handful of *Englifh-
men* to baffle the whole power of *France*;
in fuch a manner, as will make the plains
of *Minden* vie, in future ftory, with
thofe of *Agincourt* and *Creffi:* in fhort,
has enabled the foft and delicate foldier
not only to bear the common toils of
war; but has carried him fafely through
the unufual hardfhip of a winter's
campaign, in a moft inclement feafon:
whilft the poor, puny, fickly failor has,
by their falutiferous quality, been rendered

ed equal to a conflict with enemies and elements at once.*

I know it will hurt you to have so much said of the great efficacy of your writings; because you disclaim all *Panaceas*, as the very *Empiricism of Politics*. But though you don't, act like the man, who sells the *famous Pectoral Drops*, or *grand renovating Elixir of life*; stand at the corner of a street, and slip bills into our hands, with directions to the true original warehouse; yet I cannot help concluding with the poet,

Sunt verba *et* voces,——*sunt certa piacula, quæ* nos *Ter purè lecto possunt* re-creare *libello. scil. tuo.*

Which I think, now the secret is out, would not make a bad motto to the *sixteenth edition* of your book.

This indeed was a point, which you most carefully kept out of sight; and I flatter myself, I can guess the reason, why you did so. You plainly saw, that

we

---

* Alluding to Sir *Edward Hawke's* Victory.

we wanted phyfic; and yet thought, we were fo childifh, there would be no getting us to take any, if offered in the form of a pill or a bolus; (that is, under the difguftful appearance of direct advice:) and therefore you prudently intimated, you intended no fuch thing: though at the fame time you were administering the proper remedies under the pleafing vehicle of an Eftimate: when inftantly, the diforders were removed; the noxious humors paffed off; and, what is very furprizing, we had fwallowed our cure, without knowing any thing of the matter.

I am aware, it will be faid, that you have had many and able coadjutors in this matter: people, who are envious of letting one man bear away fuch a load of praife, will talk, fome of *two*, fome of ten or twenty, *Great Men*, who muft fhare this honor with you. But what fignify a parcel of names, that ferve only to fill the mouths of a mob; your *Wolfe*'s, *Hawke*'s, or *Bofcawen*'s! what
could

could theſe have done, without your
aſſiſtance? I have but one reaſon for
asking that queſtion, and I deſire no
other, it is ſo full to the purpoſe;
" They were in being before you
" wrote your book; what did they
" do *then?*"

In ſhort, when I reflect upon this, I
know not, whether I am more chagrin-
ed or ſurpriſed to obſerve, that your
ſingular merit has paſt unregarded by
the H--ſe of C----ns on this occaſion; who, whilſt they have been ſo liberal in v-t-ng thanks to many inferior actors, have never taken the leaſt
notice of the *A-th-r* of the *Eſt-m-te;*
though he appears, ſo clearly, to have
been the main-ſpring, which put the
whole machine in motion.

As far as this omiſſion can be ſup-
plied by the voice of a ſingle perſon, I
beg leave, in this public manner, to
offer you my moſt humble congratula-
tions on the great ſucceſs of your writings, — hoping, that no neglect of o-
thers

thers will deprive us of the ftill greater
benefit to be expected from your larger
Work.   I beg leave to fubfcribe myfelf,

With all the due deference,

and diftance,

Which a poor humble monofyllable,

at the bottom of one of your own pages,

obferves towards it's fuperiors,

Yours.

AN

EXPLANATION

OF THE

DESIGN of this ESTIMATE,

ADDRESSED

To the Reverend and Learned

The DEAN of LINCOLN.

SIR,

I Know no piece of vanity more common, or which perhaps is more excufable (efpecially when we are got amongft ftrangers) than to pretend an acquaintance with a perfon of fome confequence, who is generally known, and thought well of. We cannot help flattering ourfelves with the hopes, that they, in whofe company we are engaged, will immediately afcribe a part of his worth to us; and that by this means we fhall appear to them, in a more refpectable point of view: neither can it be doubted, but that if the bufinefs be properly managed, a prepoffeffion may be thus raifed in our favor, which will ferve, like a letter recommendatory;

tory; at leaft, till we, by fome mifconduct, have deftroyed it's good effect, and betrayed our own unworthinefs.

The reafon, which induced me to make ufe of your Name on this occafion, I need only tell to *you*, for every body elfe will fee of courfe, that it was an affectation of the above fort: I knew you to be one, who was a friend to learning, and indeed to every thing, that is worthy; I was therefore willing to have it thought, that you were a friend to me.

But how far I can have any pretence to your friendfhip in this inftance, is only to be feen by my declaring the defign, I have in view, and thofe confiderations, which gave rife to it.

The End then propofed in the prefent treatife, which I have ventured to lay before you and the public, Is, firft of all, " To vin-" dicate the ways of God to men," by opening to their view, in fome degree, a regular plan of his proceedings with them; from which I hope to make it appear, that there has been a continual *Tendency to the better* in all human affairs. The manner, in which I have attempted to do this, is by making the faireft Eftimate, I could, both of thofe

Prin-

Principles, under which mankind feem to have acted at different periods of their exiftence; and alfo of thofe *Manners*, which have characterifed the feveral ages of the world.

Another part of my defign is, " To enlarge men's notions a little," by offering to their confideration a fet of free and liberal fentiments, though not always immediately tending to the above principal point.

Laftly, I have endeavoured to draw a fairer picture of the *Prefent Times*, than that, offered to the public in *a late Eftimate :* not that I mean to enter into any particular examination, either of the candor or abilities fhewn in that work: an inquiry of that fort, " might juftly be regarded, as a re- " fearch rather curious, than neceffary; *fince* " (as the author well obferves, pag. 203,) *a fingle reflection on the prefent ftate of the kingdom may feem to ftand in the place of a thoufand proofs,*" ☞ That the Doctor was ——— MISTAKEN.

Men are welcome, provided they allow the defign to be good, to fay, if they think fo, that the execution is not anfwerable. I am not fo follicitous about their opinion in this refpect, as in the other: the one I could not well remedy; the other I eafily might:

and

and I know, that you and all candid judges, who are convinced of the good intention, will make all proper allowances, for the method of purfuing it. As to the faftidious and critical reader, whofe fupreme pleafure may confift in the difcovery of miftakes and inaccuracies, I fhall not trouble myfelf to befpeak his clemency and indulgence by the common pleas of hurry, avocations, &c; fince I have, in all probability, confulted his fatisfaction more, by affording materials for his fault-finding obfervation to employ itfelf upon, than I could have done, by any other means whatever.*

Many things, I am fenfible, are but flightly touched upon, which might have deferved a fuller difquifition. Others, perhaps, have been dwelt upon even to fatiety and difguft: whilft many more, which may be thought to have fome connexion with this inquiry, have been intirely omitted. This however is feemingly the cafe with moft books

---

* As I believe myfelf to be the firft, who ever made ufe of this plea, in favor of bad writing, I expect to be allowed the full benefit of it, during my fourteen years property in this book; and if I ever write another, I hope it will either ftand lefs in need of an excufe; or that I fhall have found out, by that time, a better.

books publifhed; and may therefore poffibly
be pardoned in one, confifting of fuch various materials, as the prefent; efpecially by
thofe, who confider, what a trouble it is
even to write a very indifferent book; and,
that this trouble is ufually undertaken, either for their pleafure or profit; however
the author may be deceived in his expecta-
tion. I have, in particular, entered very
fparingly into modern politics: for whatever
inclination I might have, as an *Englifhman,*
to gratify the reader on this fubject; I found,
that by having lived at a diftance from the
WORLD, though books might have furnifh-
ed me with fome general notions, I fhould
defcend to particulars with an aukward-
nefs, which would only expofe me to the ridicule of men, acquainted with AFFAIRS.*

With regard to the liberty I have taken
of throwing a part of my fentiments into
the

* It is to be hoped however, that this frank con-
feffion, will not fubject me to the *fad* mortification
of having it retorted upon me; that, for the fame
reafon, I fhould have omitted many other particulars.
Indeed, gentle reader, however I may be miftaken,
thefe particulars were *only* inferted, becaufe they
feemed to fall, if not more within my reach, at leaft
more within that province, of which I have affumed
the cognifance, than the others.

the form of notes, it was done principally
for my own eafe; but with a diftant view,
at the fame time, to that of the reader;
who, if he is fatisfied with what he meets
with in the text, need not trouble himfelf
with looking into the notes: but, if in any
matter he requires farther information, he
may perhaps fometimes find it in that part,
which is printed in a fmaller charaƐter, in
order to fave the trouble of connexion, and
at the fame time avoid embarraffment. I have
befides, now and then, when I thought myfelf
moft open to the force of banter, endeavoured to fly for refuge to a note; with what
fuccefs, can only be known from the event.

As to the plan, by which I fuppofe Providence to have aƐted; it is not offered to the
public, much lefs to you, Sir, as any new
difcovery, arifing from my own reafon or
obfervation: I own this with the greater
pleafure; as it has been already fo much
better recommended to people's attention,
by the name and writings of a far more able
advocate:* whofe excellent Difcourfe on
The Progrefs of Natural Religion and Science,
whoever reads with fufficent attention, will
have no need to come here for farther con-
viƐtion;

* Dr. *Law*, Mafter of St. *Peter's* College, *Cambridge.*

viction; nor would he, I am afraid, find it, if he did. However as * light troops are of ufe in war, as well as the more regular and embodied foldiery; fo may it alfo perhaps be of fervice, in the defence of truth, to purfue fometimes a loofer or lefs difciplined method, as well as a clofer and more correct way of reafoning.

The end propofed is certainly fuch a one, as every thinking man muft be heartily defirous of feeing fatisfactorily made out: to all of whom it cannot but have been matter of frequent concern, to reflect upon the many incongruous, abfurd, and unworthy notions; which have, from time to time, and from one end of the earth to the other, been entertained of the Deity, and his dealings with his creatures, — fo derogatory to his honor, and detrimental to their happinefs! not only by the unenlightened *Indian*, who boils and bakes the object of his worfhip; and

---

* I am well aware, that thefe troops cut but a poor figure, in " The famous battle, fought fome " years ago in St. *James*'s library;" but either nature or fate impelled me fo ftrongly, that I could not help enlifting into this very corps. — I muft therefore patiently fubmit to all the ridicule, which my conduct juftly deferves.

and whom therefore one can more readily allow to think, what he pleafes, of his own workmanfhip; but by the more rational heathen: not only by the *Monks* and *Copti's*; but by the more informed part of the chriftian world; — who have feemingly taken all the pains they could, to make " The religion of God of none effect;" — who have labored, one fhould think, only to eftablifh the truth of that prophecy of our Saviour, " That he was not come to bring peace on " earth, but a fword;" — who, as if the religion, which he taught, had been incomplete, have been ever bufy in fupplying it's defects by abfurd additions of their own; " brick, ftraw, ftubble!" which have been put together with what, in every fenfe of of the word, may be juftly called " untem-" pered morter;" — who have been continually difputing and fighting for formularies and creeds, for what men fhould believe, without troubling their heads about what they practifed. — Nay, of fo much greater importance have they judged the firft of thefe articles to be, than the latter; that, in order to teach men to believe, what they could either never know at all, or leaft never know to be right; they have fuffered, or rather

indeed

indeed taught, them to do, what they could not but know to be wrong.

By thefe means, whilft oppofite fides have been contending for the right of prefcribing to each other's confciences; frequently in matters, with which the confciences of neither had any thing at all to do; religion, that is, every thing, which deferves that name, has lain, like a litigated eftate, neglected by both parties; and in confequence of that, inftead of it's genuine fruits, when properly culti-vated, righteoufnefs and peace; has produc-ed all the evil weeds of envy, rancour, malice, and revenge.

At one time, as if the Deity could not be good, unlefs men were bad; a great deal of pains has been taken to reprefent us, as a fet of unnatural, mifhapen monfters, all vile-nefs and deformity,—contrary to the exprefs word of God himfelf; who has declared, that whatever he created, "was very good;" which furely we never can look upon, as the temporary applaufe of a day only. It would be a piece of cunning of fo low a kind, that we fhould hardly pardon it in the meaneft artificer; who, knowing, that his work-manfhip would certainly fall in pieces to-morrow, fhould feize the prefent moment to

fet

set off and exalt his extraordinary performance. How shall men dare then to ascribe any
thing, like this, to the Author of all truth
and perfection!

At another time, as if men could not be
good, unless the Deity were bad; the kind,
beneficent Father of mankind has been re-
presented, as their great enemy and de-
stroyer; has been dressed in all the fiery
robes of burning indignation, and armed
with terror and relentless fury!

How far such representations might be
necessary in the grosser ages of the world,
one cannot well pretend to determine: neither would it be easy to say, whether they
might not even still be usefully applied to
the lower class of mankind; whose dull
mind is incapable of being much affected by
any generous or exalted ideas; and who
cannot receive any lasting impressions, but
from objects, which strike the senses: this
however one may safely venture to affirm,
that the bawling methodist, who pours forth
storms of hail, fire and brimstone, upon the
ignorant, gaping, and affrighted multitude,
that attend him, and greedily drink in his
precious instructions, is more justifiable, than
the learned divine, who endeavours, in his

la-

labored volumes, to impofe an abfurd belief on the more rational part of mankind.

But what will not a blind attachment to fyftems do? In order to procure efteem and veneration for certain human eftablifhments, of worth and excellency enough, confidered merely as fuch; men have induftrioufly taken pains, and have unhappily fucceeded in their endeavours, to make them be look-ed upon, as effential parts of chriftianity it-felf; which ftrange proceeding has brought with it this very natural confequence, befides many others equally aukward; that, by it's means, the caufe of our holy religion, and the decrees of councils and fynods, (two ex-tremely different things!) have been put upon the fame iffue;— from whence we may juftly derive no fmall part of that fcepticifm and infidelity, which has lately deluged a neighbouring kingdom, and has flowed even hither:— for men, having been taught to look upon the church of Chrift and his Re-ligion to be the fame thing, and having been able to difcover fome flaws in the for-mer, have too haftily concluded, that the fame might be met with in the latter.

Things however are not quite fo bad amongft us; may we duely thank God for it!

it!—that fpirit of gentlenefs and tolerancy
in our church,—that great moderation in
claiming no abfolute authority over men's
confciences, in matters of belief, has fecured us from a great part of this mifchief: —
but even we, I doubt, have been in fome degree blameable.

That the chriftian religion at large is calculated to promote the good of mankind in
general, is not perhaps more true, than that
particular modes of it are peculiary fuited,
to advance the happinefs of particular fets
of men, united together, under certain laws,
in the fame fociety: — wherever then the
wifdom of Lawgivers has been fuch, as to
model the religion of a country in fuch a
manner, as may beft fuit the frame of government, there eftablifhed; (provided there
be in it nothing directly contrary to the
doctrine of Chrift,) and experience has
fhewn, that it is peculiarly adapted to the
genius of the inhabitants, and circumftances of the kingdom; men can fcarce too
ftrenuoufly labor to inculcate a love and
efteem for this form of worfhip among the
people.

Yet, if they go fo far as to make them believe the worth of it confifts intirely in a

par-

particular determined form of prayer, or in certain indifferent rites and ceremonies; this inconvenience will attend their zeal, — that (if afterwards, either by a change of circum-stances; by the governments having under-gone some alteration; or by a farther insight into things, it should be discovered, that some amendments might be made in this form of worship,) there will be found such an attach-ment in the common people to their old forms, that it would be extremely hazardous to risque an innovation; as ninety-nine out of a hundred of these would fancy, you were rooting up religion itself.

So that in time, when, by such alterati-ons, as the wisdom of succeeding ages would discover to be for the better, the civil go-vernment was become more and more per-fect and complete; the established religion, which should have kept pace with it, will be the most *imperfect thing in it, and per-haps

---

* Just as the holy Scriptures are likely to become the most incorrect books amongst us, by that ab-surd position, that even the words of them, being dictated, nay the very fingers of the penmen, who transcribed them, being guided, by unerring inspi-ration, they cannot admit of the ordinary rules of criticism.

haps hardly fuitable to it in it's prefent form.

There is more meaning in that diftincti-on of HIGH CHURCH and *Low Church*, fo bandied about in a late reign, than there is in moft other diftinctions, which were then, or have been fince, in ufe among us. What the learned *Montefquieu* obferves, of the popifh religion being fuited to abfolute monar-chies, and the proteftant to thofe, where li-berty is eftablifhed by law, is true in fome degree of the different forms of proteftan-tifm itfelf; fo that in a kingdom, where the prerogative of the crown has been gradu-ally leffened, and liberty better fecured, fome high-flown notions in Church policy might poffibly be lowered for the better.

But what then? Are we quietly to fit ftill, and patiently to hear the cavils of every no-vice, who pretends to find fault with what he cannot mend? Not fo neither. All that is here meant is only to recommend it, as a point of prudence, to leffen, as much as we can, the number of thofe things, that lie o-pen to the attempts of our adverfaries.

By keeping up, more for fhow, than any real ufe, large and extenfive outworks, many of which are at beft capable of but a weak

de-

defence, we do in fome fort endanger or expofe the citadel itfelf; fince our enemies
will be forward to interpret every flight advantage, which they may accidentally gain
againft one of thefe, as if it affected the
main body. Whereas, by voluntarily furren-
dering fome of the moft advanced and leaft
tenable pofts, our attention in defending the
reft would be lefs diftracted; and thefe, by
being nearer to the main work, againft
which, we are told, "the moft fiery darts of
our worft enemy fhall never be able to pre-
vail," would receive fhelter from, as well as
give ftrength to, it.

However it may be faid, that it is not
only the private œconomy of a particular
Church, which is called in queftion; but
that even the great general difpenfations of
Providence itfelf are daringly attacked. Notwithftanding the reprehenfion in the Gofpel, " Shall the thing formed, fay to him
" that formed it, why haft thou made me
" thus?" Men have ever made it their practice, and it fcarce can be doubted, but that
they ever will continue to inquire, why they
were made, as they are; and indeed with
fome fhow of reafon too, provided they can
bring themfelves to think, that their cir-

cum-

cumſtances and accommodations are not ſo good, as they might have been: the impious ridicule upon Providence, implied in the anſwer of the *Derviſe* in * *Candide,* would otherwiſe have too much foundation; "Thinkeſt thou, ſays he, when his " ſublime Highneſs ſends a veſſel to *Egypt,* " that he concerns himſelf at all, whether " the Mice on board have room or not?" " What would you have one do then, " ſaid *Pangloſs?*" "Hold your tongue, ſaid " the *Derviſe.*"

Let us ſee rather, what it is, which theſe complainers would have; and how far it may appear to have been in the power of their Creator to ſatisfy them. To ſpeak according to the narrowneſs of our ideas, there ſeems

to

* The Author of this profane piece of burleſque, has raked together all the little circumſtances, that ſeem to throw a ſhade upon God's moral government, many of which ariſe merely from the neceſſary imperfection of human governments and inſtitutions; and even theſe he has been mean enough to miſrepreſent: by ſuch low artifice has he attempted to laugh us out of the belief of a divine ſuperintendency: his attempt would have been juſt as wiſe, had he endeavoured to prove, that the Sun did not ſhine, becauſe an accidental cloud or eclipſe may ſometimes intervene, and for a while intercept a part of it's brightneſs from our view.

to have been only two things in the choice
of the Deity, when he determined to create
Mankind; either to place them in a certain
fubordinate degree of happinefs, with powers to promote themfelves to higher degrees;
or to have given them the higheft poffible
happinefs at once : which laft, it is likely,
is the very thing, which they, who are dif-
fatisfied with their prefent condition, long
for; but which, if carefully attended to,
will perhaps be found to be an impoffible
cafe; for it feemingly implies a contradiction, even for infinite power itfelf to make
any pofitive degree of happinefs, how great
foever, the greateft poffible,—between what is
infinite, and the next ftep to it, there muft
always be an immeafurable void, which will
ever afford room for the fuppofition of going farther and farther, without coming at
all to any determinate end:—fo that the only
way, which our beneficent Creator had of
communicating the greateft happinefs to his
Creatures, was by fetting no bounds to it,
but allowing us to go on from one degree
to another, in an endlefs progreffion. Had
the Deity placed us in any fixed, determined
degree of happinefs, with underftanding e-
nough to fee, that there might be higher degrees,

grees, we fhould have been lofers by this ap‐ pointment.

If it be ftill faid, that, even allowing this progreffive ftate to be the beft,we might have fet out from a higher ftep in the fcale; it might be anfwered, that wherever the firft ftep was taken, there would lie the fame matter of complaint againft it, as againft the prefent.

In fact, if we were to be placed in a ftate of morality; that is, in fuch a ftate, as to be able, by our own choice, to become the au‐ thors of our own happinefs or mifery; fuch an allotment of things, as at prefent obtains, feems in fome fort neceffary; where the ba‐ lance is pretty near equally fufpended : fo that there fhould be no great force upon the will, or prepollency in favor of one fide, more than the other.— All that is wanting, or can be defired in fuch a ftate, is, that the proportion of good may appear fo fuf‐ ficiently above the bad, that we may with reafon conclude, the Deity had our happi‐ nefs in view at creation: — and if it fhould be farther evident, that this happinefs is growing daily greater; we have the faireft argument, which analogy can afford, that it will continue for ever to do fo : which is alfo greatly ftrengthened by that ftretch and

ten-

tendency, which every one muſt experience in his mind, to get forward; by that appetency after future things, that graſping after happineſs, that lies ſtill beyond our reach; which certainly was never implanted in our nature merely to mock and diſappoint us.

The caſe however of thoſe, who may abuſe their liberty of choice to their own deſtruction, may ſtill ſeem to ſtand in our way: if the number of theſe ſhould be greater, or indeed bear any conſiderable proportion to thoſe, who uſe their freedom rightly; it may afford ſome plauſible matter for objection to thoſe, who would impeach the goodneſs of their Maker, — as if he had acted contrary to that goodneſs, in placing his creatures in ſuch precarious circumſtances, as he muſt know before-hand would prove the occaſion of falling to ſo many.

Now we may obſerve by the way, that in whatever circumſtances the Deity had placed us; unleſs he had made us mere neceſſary agents, (if ſuch two terms can agree) a poſſibility of falling muſt ever have been annexed to our condition: — and "as "all ſcripture is written for our admonition," perhaps the ſtory of *Adam* in paradiſe, and that of the fallen Angels too might both be

c delivered

delivered with this view, to inform us, that we might have forfeited our happinefs, however innocent we were at firft, or how high foever, in the fcale of Beings, our rank had been affigned us.

But ftill that God fhould create any Beings upon fuch terms, as that many of them fhould become infinitely and eternally miferable, may not feem fo eafy to be got over; or reconciled to our notions of his goodnefs.

This indeed is a *hard faying*; and, unlefs the fcriptures be abfolute in enjoining the belief of it, " who would willingly receive it ?" When one confiders, how very few of our actions are in themfelves grofsly finful; how almoft all of them borrow their heinous quality, merely from their being detrimental to the happinefs of our fellow-creatures; which God was willing by all means to fecure: and when one farther confiders, for how fmall a pittance of time the worft of our actions, even murder itfelf, (which feems to be the higheft crime we are capable of committing,) will probably interrupt the happinefs of our brother; our reafon reluctantly concludes, that the punifhment of fin will be ftrictly eternal. — That there fhould be a diftinction made hereafter between

the

the good and bad; and that the latter fhould be punifhed for their mifdeeds; reafon, fcripture, every thing, calls aloud for: —but humanity enforces us to wifh, that all fuffering may tend to the reformation of the fufferers; and that, even in punifhment, " God would remember mercy!"

It is eafy to reply to this way of talking; that it proceeds rather from confcious guilt and fearful apprehenfions, than from unprejudiced conclufions: but furely it is better even to err that way, than for human arrogance to lift itfelf fo high, as impioufly to condemn men with more rigour, than God has condemned them, and daringly to confign over to everlafting perdition thofe, whom God may have created to be ultimately happy: — furely he who has goodnefs enough to declare himfelf willing, that " None fhould perifh, but that all fhould be " faved," has alfo wifdom enough to contrive the means of this, though they are fitly hid from us at prefent.

Perhaps, if it had received any countenance from fcripture, fomething like the doctrine of *Pythagoras* would have eafily recommended itfelf to our belief: for, that nothing, which has once tafted the blefsing

of

of exiftence, will ever intirely ceafe to be, is a principle highly agreeable to our reafon; as we cannot well conceive any other motive for it's firft creation, than the Deity's willing it to be happy: and as there is " no varia- " blenefs, nor fhadow of turning in him," we might therefore conclude, that the fame motive would ever retain it's full force.

Suppofing then exiftence not to be loft, of what import can it be, (provided this is not brought about by any finful act,) that it's courfe may accidentally be diverted into another channel, where it will flow on with lefs interruption?

Beings of a day, as we are, can form but imperfect notions of fuch vaft defigns, as are and have been, the bufinefs of eternity. Notwithftanding our boafted privilege of *looking before and after*; all, we can clearly fee, is juft the narrow fpot, that lies around us; one fcene perhaps, or lefs of the great drama, in which " all mankind are merely " players, as the poet calls them, who have " their exits and their entries;" and it mat- ters not at all, whether one man has a longer part in this fcene than another, as they will both fo foon quit it to enter on the next: and we muft ftay the conclud- ing

ing act to know, whether exact poetic juftice has been done or not; enough for us, if we can in the mean time learn from what has paft, what is moft likely to be hereafter: if we can fee juft a diftant open- ing of the plot, enough to lead us to guefs with probability at the Cataftrophe.

If then from thofe parts, which have been already acted, we can difcover *a Tendency to the better* in things; we may reft fatisfied, and fafely conclude, that they will for ever go on in the fame way. And that there is fuch *a ten- dency*, will, it is hoped, appear from the fol- lowing Eftimate. Not but it muft be owned, there are many intricacies, which embarrafs this plan: — though perhaps no difficulty, which ftands in the way, is fo hard to be got over, as to perfuade people to think as well of thofe things, of which "familiarity, " according to the old proverb, has bred a " contempt,"* as of thofe, which they only there-

---

* To ufe a familiar inftance; how hardly do we bring ourfelves to think, that Tom, Dick, or Harry, whom we remember boys, are grown even to be men; much more men of any confequence? Unlefs, by fome means, they have been removed, for a time, from our fight and obfervation. And if it may be allowable to add an inftance of much higher impor-

tance;

therefore admire, becaufe they cannot fee, clearly, what they are.

I am afraid, Sir, you will look upon this Addrefs, as already carried to too great a, length; yet, before I conclude it, I muft beg leave to obferve, that whatever becomes of the argument, when extended to the world at large; it muft affect every lover of fcience, and friend to this place, with the fincereft pleafure to think, that it is moft, ftrictly true, when applied to the ftate of this Univerfity: which is not more vifibly im-, proved in the outward appearance of it's, ftructures and public buildings, than in the learning and manners of it's inhabitants. The minds of youth were never taught to think with a more becoming freedom; the, only way, by which they can be taught to think right; or more ftrongly impreffed with lively fentiments of true chriftian hu-, manity; that is, a proper confideration of their

tance; we know, that the greateft character, which ever adorned human nature, found no honor in his own country : " Is not this the carpenter's fon ; are " not his brethren and his fifters with us :" were arguments enough to induce men to believe, that he ought not to pretend to know more, than they did. On the other hand, how eafily, and how conftantly, are we bubbled by any foreign impoftor? — But thefe confiderations, belong more properly to another place.

their own and other people's happineſs; which probably conſtitutes both the end and means of all true religion; and ſeems to be the only impreſſion, which, conſiſtently with a free uſe of reaſon, can be ſtampt upon the mind, before it has attained the power of judging for itſelf. In conſequence of this, there never was a time, when this *nurfing* MOTHER of ſcience could boaſt of ſo many ſons, who were poſſeſſed of ſo much real and uſeful knowledge, or who practiſed more rational or more civilized manners; eſpeci-ally among that part of them, who by their birth and fortune throw a ſplendor and dig-nity upon learning; who always ſhould endeavour, and who uſually have it in their power, to make a greater progreſs in ſcience, than others: theſe have lately in a more particular manner made it their ſtudy to ex-cel in this, as they already do in all other advantages.*

Without

---

* It certainly is much to be wiſhed, that the plan of education here were ſo enlarged, (if it could be conſiſtently with the main end of our inſtitution, the ſending out into the world an able ſupply of men for the ſacred Miniſtry,) as to induce young men of family and fortune to reſide longer amongſt us, than for the two or three early years, which u-ſually bound their ſtay here. How much better

would

Without entering more minutely into the causes of this, we might appeal for a confirmation of the truth of it to every one, who is at all acquainted with our situation; whatever some, who live at a * distance, have, on that account, imagined to the contrary.

" With

would this be, both for the community and themselves, than to have them almost under a necessity of going to some foreign University; where, however they may learn a more polite address, or other such like accomplishments, they certainly cannot learn more true knowledge?

* We might therefore easily be excused from giving any particular answer to them, if they had not received one already.+ But at the same time, it must be owned, that a person of much greater consequence, than they; even the great Lord *Bacon*, who was in fact, what he, with more compliment, than truth, said of *Plato*, " Vir sublimis ingenii, qui- " que veluti ex rupe excelsâ omnia circumspicie- " bat," has bent his thoughts toward our institutions, and has left us the following observation upon them : " *Defectus* etiamnum alius nobis observan- " dus, magni certè momenti, neglectus quidam est, " in Academiarum rectoribus, consultationis; in re- " gibus sive superioribus, visitationis; in hunc fi- " nem, ut diligenter consideretur et perpendatur, " utrum prælectiones, disputationes, aliaque exer- " citia scholastica, antiquitus instituta et ad nostra " usque tempora usitata, continuare fuerit ex usu, " vel potius antiquare, aliaque meliora substituere. " Etenim inter Majestatis tuæ (*Jacobi* 1ᵐⁱ) canones " prudentissimos illum reperio. *In omni vel consue-* " tudine.

+ See O*bservations on the Present state of the* English *Universi- ties, Occasioned by Dr.* Davies's *Account of the Education in them.*

With what gratitude then must we needs look upon those, who, by their liberality and

" *tudine vel exemplo, tempora spectanda sunt, quando*
" *primum res cœpta : in quibus si vel confusio regna-*
" *verit vel inscitia, derogat illud imprimis authoritati*
" *rerum, atque omnia suspecta reddit.* Quamobrem,
" quandoquidem Academiarum instituta plerum-
" que originem traxerint a temporibus *hisce nostris*
" haud paulo obscurioribus, et indoctioribus ; eo
" magis convenit, ut examini denuo subjiciantur. "
How far this might be intended to flatter that pe-
dantic Monarch, of whose wisdom we have a speci-
men here given us, and who was always fond of having a hand in every thing, that related to religion or
learning, may perhaps be difficult to determine : but
that, what is said, is founded in truth, can admit of
no dispute. Time, and the prudence of more modern Ages, may, and no doubt have greatly lessen-
ed the number of those things, which were formerly
liable to exception. Yet he might be suspected of
having more partiality, than sincere judgement, who
should undertake to say, that nothing of this sort
was now to be found amongst us. However it may
best become us to leave these matters to the conside-
ration of those, to whom the above-cited, great Author committed them. If, in the mean time, a private person may be indulged a wish upon the sub-
ject; mine should be, that the way to *Natural Knowledge* was rendered a little more easy amongst us, by
having a supply given us of such things, as our
slender incomes ill enable us to purchase ourselves.
Our Schools should be furnished with good appara-
tus's for observations and experiments. Ample Sti-
pends should be allotted to our Professors of A-
natomy, Chemistry, and Botany ; the whole to be
forfeited on their ceasing to read Lectures, which
should

and attention to our welfare, have afforded the means of thefe improvements ; efpecially on

fhould all be *Gratis*. And a Laboratory fhould be eftablifhed, and endowed with a fufficient revenue to pay inferior Operators for their attendance, and alfo for fupplying proper utenfils and materials for going through a courfe of Chemiftry ; where every one of the Univerfity, whofe turn led him that way, might have free accefs to make, what trials he pleafed. What would have made another part of this wifh is already, it feems, in a fair way of being anfwered by our being upon the point of having a Phyfic Garden eftablifhed, through the munificence of a very worthy Member of this place, Dr. *Walker* of *Trinity College*. And we already by a former benefaction have an exceeding good collection of Foffils, and a handfome appointment for a Lecturer.

It might not be abfurd perhaps to add the following wifh to the former, though about a matter of much lefs confequence ; — That all our public Difputations, were carried on in our own Language, and in a lefs confined way than that of fyllogifms. People would blufh at that nonfenfe, when cloathed in plain *Englifh*, which affumes an air of importance, and even challenges refpect, when dreffed in very indifferent *Latin*. We might too, by this means, learn in time to talk in our own Tongue, with eafe and elegance, inftead of mangling and maiming another, which, at laft, we fhall fpeak but very imperfectly.

Wifhes however, I am fenfible are, at beft, both exceeding flow Benefactors, and to the full as idle Reformers ! Poffibly too, many a prudent man may fhake his head at fuch empty things, as vifionary projectors only dream of ; and many a good one may fatisfy himfelf, that there cannot be much reformation wanting in thofe inftitutions, which have
always

on one great * Man, who has long been the liberal encourager and patron of every thing, which

always hitherto anfwered the ends, they were defign-ed for : whilft many more may fancy, that it does not much fignify, how fuch places, as thefe, are or-dered, or regulated : — that the great matter is, to bring Men of letters together, who, like *Bees*, will do all the reft, that is expeƈted from them of courfe.

Principio fedes Apibus, ftatioque petenda,
Quo neque fit ventis aditus, &c.

Now this may be, and probably is the principal thing; when you have already got Men of letters fit, and prepared to enter upon their feveral different purfuits and employments ; juft as we fee it happen, about the Capitals of Kingdoms and other large Ci-ties ; where, without any other encouragement, than the mere friendly intercourfe of Arts and Sciences with each other, the greateft progrefs in Learning is daily made. But the queftion at prefent is, how we fhall be moft likely to raife men of Learning, — whether by following that method, which was chalk-ed out to us in very ignorant Ages, when almoft all the knowledge in the world was fhut up in *Greek* and *Latin*, and was only to be acquired by a pre-vious infight into their idioms, and phrafes ; or whe-ther we fhould look out for fome new one now, when circumftances are intirely changed ; and not go on to wafte the beft part of our time and attention in gaining an acquaintance with thofe Languages, which, when underftood, will not furnifh us with half the knowledge to be met with in our own ; not but, however it's ufe may ceafe, it muft always continue to be matter of the higheft entertainment, as well as ornament too to the Scholar, to be able to read the wifdom of former Ages, in thofe Lan-guages, in which it was originally wrote.

* Our CHANCELLOR.

which might tend to raife the reputation of this our *Athens?*

After thefe, they claim the next fhare of our praife, by whofe prudent management, the beneficence of others has been made to anfwer the end, it was defigned for: amongft the firft of which number, the DEAN of LINCOLN's Name, if I fhould omit it, cannot fail to be reckoned by every body elfe.

I am,

SIR,

Your moft obliged,

and moft obedient,

humble Servant,

CAMBRIDGE,
March 20. 1760.

The AUTHOR.

PART. I.

CHAP. I.
INTRODUCTION.

CHAP. II.

CHAP. III.

CHAP. IV.

CHAP. V.

PART.

CONTENTS.

PART II.

CHAP.

CONTENTS.

CHAP. VIII.

CHAP. IX.

CHAP. X.

ADVERTISEMENT.

☞ *What is here offered to the public makes only a part of the Author's Design: but this being his first Introduction to the Reader, he was not willing to make the visit of Ceremony too long. — Speedily however will be published Parts the third and fourth of this Estimate, on the Happiness and Virtue of Mankind; in which Mr. Rousseau's opinions will be particularly considered: and Part the fifth, which will be an Application of the whole to our own Times and Circumstances.*

A NEW
ESTIMATE
OF
MANNERS and PRINCIPLES.

PART I.

IN WHICH
Some common Opinions and Prejudices
are confidered.

Moft humbly,

and moft dutifully,

infcribed

to Him who deferves the following Compliment,
more than ever *Cæfar* did.

Sed Tuus *hoc populus fapiens et juftus in uno*
Te *noftris ducibus,* Te Graiis *anteferendo,*
C*ætera nequaquam fimili ratione modoque*
Æftimat ; *et nifi quæ terris femota, fuifque*
Temporibus defuncta videt, faftidit et odit.

HOR. Ep. 1. Lib. 2.

A

A NEW

ESTIMATE

OF

MANNERS and PRINCIPLES.

CHAP. I.

INTRODUCTION.

IT has now been fo long the practice to cry up the excellence of former times, and to lament modern degeneracy, that an attempt to introduce a different rule of judging muft expect to meet with no very favorable reception. Opinions of long eftablifhment in the world, like old cuftoms, acquire fo much fanctity, that whoever does not pay the moft reverential regard to them, is fure to be looked upon with an eye of jealoufy and diftruft, as if he were intending no good to mankind.

They efpecially, who, being either unable or unwilling to judge for themfelves, fuit

their

their opinions, as they do their clothes, to
the faſhion of the times, are apt to be ex-
ceedingly alarmed at any innovation; which,
conſidering the ſmall trouble an alteration
of this ſort can coſt them, one would hardly expect: but true and genuine prejudice,
being, both by nature and habit, nearly related to the old carrier's horſe, will for ever
follow the bells of it's leader; and is ſo ac-
cuſtomed to plod on, at the ſame dull rate,
and in the ſame miry path, after others;
that it is odds, but it will, right obſtinately,
kick at him, who ſhall pretend to direct it
better, or to interfere at all with it's ſacred,
hereditary right of going on, unmoleſted,
in the wrong itſelf; and of leading as
many after it, as it can, into the ſame
miſtakes.

Indeed I am not well ſatisfied, how far
it is either right for one man to interrupt
another in the quiet poſſeſſion of his opinion, or reaſonable to expect a peaceable
ſubmiſſion in this caſe. For there grows up
ſuch a tender connexion between the mind
and a favorite notion, once received, that
the moſt ingenuous frequently find a ſtrong
reluctance againſt parting with it.

But

But certainly if ever this be right or rea-
fonable, it is fo, when a change will mani-
feftly be for the better ; when we attempt
to difperfe the gloom of melancholy and
fuperftition, and in it's ftead open to the
mind a more agreeable profpect. Neither
can it be unwarrantable, one fhould think,
with fuch an end in view, efpecially when
there is likely to be no fmall degree of prejudice againft us, fhould we endeavour to
raife a little favorable partiality on our own
fide. One may furely venture therefore, without being fufpected of dealing unfairly, to
fuggeft, at fetting out, that it is much more
a man's intereft to think well of prefent times
and circumftances, in which his own lot
of life is caft, than of any paft period, in
which he can have no concern; and that
every one, who defires to be happy, fhould
wifh at leaft, it might be true, that he
was more likely to be fo now, than he
could have been, had he lived at any other
time.

They, however, who fee and think for
themfelves, and do not take their opinions
from others, as they find them ready made
up by the voice of the generality, will have
no need of fuch a wifh to help them forward

in concluding, " That the world is, and has been continually from the firſt notice we have of it, in a ſtate of improvement, with regard to every thing, that can be thought to raiſe or dignify our nature ; and that conſequently, it is now in all reſpects of that ſort, better than it ever was before:" to all ſuch as theſe, a clear ſtate of matter of fact and fair deduction from it, will, I make no doubt, evidently evince this truth.

But as the number of ſuch men is very ſmall, and as the contrary opinion, from the long poſſeſſion it has had of their minds, may have left ſome ill impreſſions even on thoſe, who are the beſt diſpoſed to receive truth; it may not, perhaps, be amiſs, before we proceed to a more direct inquiry into this ſubject, to beſtow a little time in tracing out thoſe cauſes, which have given riſe to the common notion, " That virtue, and with it happineſs, the arts, and in ſhort, every thing which gives a grace and dignity to life, has long been upon the decline."

CHAP.

CHAP. II.

In which some reasons are assigned, why men have been so generally of opinion, that the world has been growing worse, and their fallacy shewn.

ONE of the principal reasons for this opinion seems to have been the unfair comparison, which is usually made between present virtues and vices, and those which are past.

Do we not hear of more vices being practised now than formerly were, and fewer virtues? is a question, which almost every one is ready to ask: and from thence it is an easy step to the conclusion, " That consequently the manners of men are plainly in a state of degeneracy ;" which, if need were, there is the authority of a * Poet ready at hand

* Who is now one of those venerable ancients, to whom such an universal homage is paid : who however, when he himself was a modern, did not seem much inclin'd to pay it to his predecessors ; at least, if he gave up to them the point of virtue, he was by no means disposed to resign the praise of learning also ; as we may see from those lines of his quoted at the beginning of this Essay, and others from the same place.

hand to confirm, who thus complains of injurious time,

> *Damnoſa quid non imminuit dies?*
> *Ætas parentum, pejor avis, tulit*
> *Nos nequiores, mox daturos*
> *Progeniem vitioſiorem.*

If the world has been really making a
continual progreſs to greater degrees of perfection, how is it poſſible, that men ſhould
ſo far overlook it's advances, as to think and
ſay, it has been daily growing worſe? In
what light are we to look upon thoſe improvements, which ſo far from becoming
matter of common obſervation, have not
been viſible enough to prevent a concluſion,
which intirely overthrows the very ſuppoſition of their exiſtence?

This may paſs with ſome for very plauſible
arguing; but it will be found, perhaps, on due
inquiry, to have in fact no other foundation
than this; we feel the ill effects of preſent
vices, and therefore they excite in us ſtrong
emotions of indignation; whereas we can look
at thoſe, which are paſt, as unmoved, as we
are unhurt by them.

Neither let any one think it a ſufficient
reply to this, to ſay, " That for the ſame
reaſon

reafon we fhould eftimate alfo at a higher rate prefent virtues, as we are in like manner immediately fenfible of their good effects:" which if we did, it muft be owned, we fhould ftill keep the balance fair and even. But unluckily, the * propofition which afferts, "That we are more ftrongly affected by what we fee and feel, than by what we hear or read of, is only true in a partial refpect;" as we fhall find by attending to the different procefs, which virtue and vice make in our affections.

Actions, that fhock us, do indeed affect us more by happening in our own time, in our own country, and in our own neighbourhood, than when they happen at a diftance: as we are by this means made acquainted with many little circumftances, that increafe our horror, but yet are too trivial for hiftory or relation to particularife, which generally give us things only in the grofs. But it is not equally true, that thofe of a better kind affect us in the fame manner. In the cafe of prefent vices we tremble for our friends,

---

* According to the fame Poet,

*Segnius irritant animos demiffa per aures,
Quam quæ funt oculis fubjecta fidelibus ——.*

friends, our families, and ourſelves : and as
ſcarce any one thinks himſelf concerned to
extenuate their heinous quality, except the
actors of them, or their aſſociates, for whom
it is uſually dangerous too, and always of
little conſequence to appear in the defence;
they receive no alleviation, but ſuch as time
brings, which commonly blots out ſome of
the worſt circumſtances attending them.
People too, when the danger is over, begin
with greater calmneſs to conſider things, and
make allowances ; till at length, crimes of
the blackeſt hue loſe their moſt frightful
features, and appear with a ſofter aſpect, and
a fairer complexion.

The proceſs is by no means the ſame with
reſpect to good actions : as the former, when
preſent, are more ſhocking ; ſo, in the ſame
circumſtances, the latter appear leſs ſtriking. It has long ago been diſcovered, tho' not
ſufficiently attended to, " That * virtue, inſtead of affording greater pleaſure the nearer
it comes to our view, has a ſtrange kind
of property to hurt the eye of the immediate
beholder, and is ſcarce ever ſeen in it's full
beauty and perfection, but through the me-
dium

---

* *Virtutem incolumem odimus,* &c. ⸺
Urit enim fulgore ſuo, &c.

dium of hiftory : " this gives a fhape and roundnefs to it, which on account of the blaze it occafions, prefent beholders cannot fo well diftinguifh.

Envy too, and a thoufand other circum-ftances, fuch as party-quarrels and family-connexions, ftep in between the living man of worth, and his due commendation ; but, when he is once gone; has removed the hat-ed obftacle, which ftood in his rival's way to greatnefs; to make him amends for their former niggardly and unwilling allowance of that honor, which his merits might have juftly claimed, men are eager to heap even unmerited praifes on his memory; efpecially, as they are but too apt to hope, they fhall by this means leffen the pretenfions of thofe, who on the prefent ftage are treading after him in the path of glory.

It is a cruel difcouragement to the pro-feffors of virtue, the chief of whofe rewards are placed at a diftance, and are only to be come at through a road of difficulties; that thofe which lie nearer, and fhould be given to animate them in their noble pur-fuits, are ufually with-held, till they, who fhould receive them, are now become infen-fible of their worth. How much more rea-

fonably

ſonably ſhould we act, how much more our intereſt, as well as duty, would it be, to beſtow our praiſes on thoſe, who are doing preſent credit, and preſent ſervice to mankind, and who would be affected by them, than on thoſe, who, however worthy they may have been, are long ſince loſt to us, and to our praiſes too ? *

But as things are too frequently managed, the man who endeavours to excel, who would attain to any diſtinguiſhed eminence, inſtead of the animating voice of praiſe, will hear many a mortifying reflexion; inſtead of

any

* In this point of view how worthy of our regard and applauſe are they, who, by the appointment of premiums, or any other means, endeavour to excite a zeal for invention and improvement? The Worſhipful the Society of Antiquarians muſt pardon me, if I ſay, that ſuch a ſpirit is much more beneficial to mankind, than that of ſome others amongſt us, who have ſeemingly taken a vow not to like any thing that is modern ; but make it their conſtant buſineſs to ſhew, how much we are outdone in almoſt every thing by the ancients ; the ſcattered reliques of whoſe knowledge they are daily buſy in collecting: and pay as much adoration to them, as certain devotees do to reliques of another ſort. Not but that even theſe men might do the world good ſervice, would they, as they ought, be content, like the workmen at Herculaneum, with merely digging up the remains of ancient art, or repreſenting them

fairly

any help to fmooth the rugged paffage, and render his arduous attempt the eafier, will find many an ugly rub, purpofely thrown in his way; and, inftead of any friendly hand ftretched out to fave him from the danger of a falfe ftep, will feel many an adverfe pufh from thofe who ftand around him; and who, being incapable of getting higher them-felves, do therefore purpofely place as many obftacles, as they can, in the way of others; hoping, by fuch means, to keep them down, if poffible, even below the level of that fitu-ation, to which they themfelves have with diffi-

fairly to others; and not think it neceffary to de-fpife the beft productions of the modern fcholar, or artificer, in comparifon with a parcel of rufty trifies, and impaired worm-eaten nonfenfe, which is in fact juft fo much the better for not being more intire. One would almoft be inclined to think, that they had underftood *Lucretius* literally, and believed

——————————— *duntaxat oriri*
Poffe ex non-fenfu fenfum,

fo much more pleafure do they feem to take in giv-ing a meaning to what had none before, than in reading what is plain and intelligible. But it is ge-nerally too true, that

— *Saliare Numæ carmen* qui *laudat, et illud*
Quod mecum ignorat, folus volt fcire videri;
Ingeniis non ille *favet plauditque fepultis,*
Noftra fed impugnat, nos noftraque lividus odit.

difficulty clambered up; or, at leaſt, to prevent their gaining any height above them.

It muſt indeed be owned, that the beſt of
charaɛters contain ſome blemiſhes, which a
too narrow ſcrutiny may diſcover. There is
a diſtance, at which real life ſhould be look'd
at, as well as it's copy on the canvaſs: we
ſhould know before-hand, that there are
imperfeɛtions in the one, as well as in the
other, which will not bear too near or too
curious an examination; and we ſhould therefore make the ſame allowances to both. The
misfortune is, we are aware we ſhall deſtroy
our pleaſure, if we do not place the painting in the moſt advantageous point of view.
we can; whereas, I am afraid, it conſtitutes
a part of that pleaſure, to view the real man
in his worſt proportions: and for this, without going to the utmoſt ſeverity of criticiſm,
the too great nearneſs of all living charaɛters
affords too much opportunity.

But the caſe is altered, when hiſtory has
taken the honors of the dead under it's pro-
teɛtion: this, in * proportion as it is written

* Whoever reads a hiſtory, which takes in a conſiderable length of time, and will attend to the manner of drawing charaɛters uſed at the different periods of it, will ſee this exemplified in a thouſand inſtances;

4

ten at a farther diftance from the time
when a great man lived, clears off more and
more of that obloquy and detraction which
fullied his living glory. Thofe fpots, which
feen

ftances; he would fee it in all, but that the hiftorian
has fometimes a private view, by faying more or lefs
of an eminent man than he deferves, to favor fome
particular party or faction of his own times. All early
accounts too (whether they relate to the world at
large, or to the origin of particular kingdoms) being neceffarily imperfect, and hiftorians loving to
give us things complete, the beginnings of almoft all
hiftories are but fo many poetic fictions, calculated
either to compliment that ftate which gave the
Author birth, or to raife in us certain fublime notions
of the grandeur and importance of human affairs,
very different from what matter of fact would ever
have fuggefted. This one of the moft fenfible antient
hiftorians exprefsly owns, " Quæ ante conditam
" condendamve urbem, poeticis magis decora fa-
" bulis, quam incorruptis rerum geftarum monu-
" mentis traduntur, ea nec affirmare, nec refellere,
" in animo eft. Datur hæc venia antiquitati, ut mif-
" cendo humana divinis, primordia urbium auguf-
" tiora faciat." And with how favorable a prepoffeffion to antient times he himfelf fets out, may be
collected from thefe and other words in his preface;
" Ego contra hoc quoque laboris præmium petam,
" uti me a confpectu malorum, quæ noftra tot per
" annos vidit ætas, trantifper certè dum prifca illa
" *tota mente* repeto, avertam." And yet what worfe
combination of human actions could even imagination form, than that, which feems, even from his
own account, to have gone towards the firft eftablifhment of Roman greatnefs?

ſeen too nearly, intercepted ſo much of his true brightneſs, in this new poſition gradually diſappear; till at length, there is nothing left, but the fair and amiable picture of his virtue; which muſt always ſtrike when viewed in it's true light: and if it has the farther good fortune to fall into a poet's hands, it is ſet off, and adorned with every grace, that may give it a ſuperior luſtre; with every ſtroke and touch of art, that may attract attention, or win admiration from all who ſee it.

It is from hence only, that we look for perfect characters in diſtant times and diſtant countries. — It is from hence only, that the illuſtrious heroes of our own time and country, admired and gazed at by all mankind beſide; feared, and even honored by our enemies, are ſo long in gaining their juſt applauſe at home. — It is on this account, that the name of *George* or *William* does not raiſe in us an idea of ſo much greatneſs, as that of *Henry* or of *Edward* does; and even theſe great names themſelves muſt, for the ſame reaſon, in their turn, yield to the ſuperior ſounds of *Scipio* and *Cæſar.*

CHAP.

CHAP. III.

Containing some other reasons to the same purpose.

TO the confiderations, mentioned in the foregoing chapter, as likely to induce men to think worfe of the prefent, and better of former times, than either might deferve; may be added the propenfity, which there has ever been in old men, " to praife the times *paffed,* when they were young," and to prefer them to the prefent; the former of which may eafily appear more agreeable to them, than the latter, without being fo in fact; fince the great difference is, moft probably, only in themfelves. They were then naturally difpofed to think the beft of every thing; their health and fpirits gave a higher relifh to their pleafures, which they had but few cares to interfere with; above attending to confequences, they enjoyed the prefent moment free from any impertinent interruption of thought and reflexion; ready to employ every idle hour (as the poet has it,) " With fomething new to wifh, or to enjoy," they would have little leifure, and ftill lefs inclination, to make any fevere fcrutiny into what might be amifs; indeed if they had

B   both,

both, they muſt be extremely ill-qualified for the undertaking, having as yet had no opportunity for obſervation and compariſon, which alone could enable them to form any true judgement.

It is well, if age and infirmities have not altered their diſpoſition; it is well, if they be not now peeviſh and fretful; hard to be pleaſed; ſoon out of humor; rigid and ſevere in their cenſures; which to juſtify, they may be willing to have it thought, that ſuch was the world in their time, it would have afforded no occaſion for theſe complaints.

Or, to put the caſe more favorably for them, being now arrived to a nearer proſpect of better pleaſures, and having in a great meaſure loſt thoſe paſſions, which ſtamped a value upon inferior enjoyments; it is no wonder, if they now begin to deſpiſe theſe, which yet, they may remember, they once held in the higheſt eſtimation; and may therefore conclude, if they do not attend to what has paſſed within themſelves in the mean time, that not they, but theſe are altered and abated in their worth. Which ever way it is, if we are at all influenced in forming our judgement by their authority, we ſhall in all probability, make a wrong one;

as they are fo very liable to be prejudiced in their reprefentations.

We may farther take into this fame account the univerfal practice of the Poets, which has ever been uniform in favor of early times; the neceffary fimplicity, frugality, and temperance of which, have been the fineft fubjects imaginable for them to difplay their fancy upon, when they had a mind to paint the virtues of mankind, and give us the picture of a golden age: whereas, on the other hand, all their fatyr has neceffarily been always pointed at times prefent; which, otherwife, would lofe it's edge and poignancy.

It is for this reafon, that the writers, of Farce and Comedy only, prefent us with living characters; whereas the Tragedians, and Epic poets travel in fearch of their's into the remoteft antiquity: for, it being the bufinefs of the firft to reprefent men, as they are, with a large mixture of imperfection always, and often of ridicule belonging to them; their end is beft anfwered by giving us fuch defcriptions, as are moft fuitable to what we daily fee, and converfe with. But the aim of the other being to reprefent men, as they neither do, nor ever did exift;

to

to give us certain complete patterns of virtue and perfection; they muſt needs endeavour to lay their ſcenes at as great a diſtance, as they can, that the improbability
may not ſhock us too much by an immediate
compariſon; and the farther they get out of
ſight, for this reaſon, the better it is; for
their characters being merely, or in a great
meaſure, fictitious, if they did not throw
them much into ſhade, the impoſition would
be too viſible and glaring: being thus forced
to have recourſe to Antiquity, they have
taken care amply to repay the aſſiſtance,
they derived from it, by beſtowing upon it in
return the higheſt encomiums they could.

This however, we may obſerve, is as true
of thoſe we call Antients, as of the Moderns;
for though *Ariſtophanes, Terence,* and *Moliere,*
all preſent us with characters of the times,
in which they wrote; yet *Sophocles* and *Euripides* no more deſcribe the actions of living
Heroes, than * *Shakeſpear* or *Corneille.*

It

---

* Conſidered as a Tragedian.

And *Horace* was ſo convinced of the neceſſity of
this practice, that, in his advice to the Tragedian,
he lays it down for a rule,

Rectius Iliacum carmen deducis in Actus,

Quam ſi proferres ignota indictaque *primus.*

That is, you had better take any ancient ſtory for the
ſubject of your play, than a modern event, which
may

It may be worth notice here, in paffing, that though all thefe authors defcribe charac-ters of paft ages, yet they muft be fuppofed to have drawn their ideas of thofe virtues, which they deck them out with, from the age, in which they themfelves lived. If this be true, how infinitely do the moderns ex-cell

may be yet in a great meafure unknown to the ge-nerality of mankind, and has received no eftablifhed reputation by being chronicled in the facred page of hiftory or poetry;—and he gives this reafon for it,

Difficile eft proprè communia dicere. —

Which with the leave of Critics, who have given a different interpretation of it, I would conftrue thus, " it is difficult to give a propriety or dignity to occurrences of common life," however diftrefsful, which have not yet been fingled out, and fet up for men to gaze and wonder at.

This is farther confirmed by another direction which he gives his young author, prefaced in the following manner,

Siquid inexpertum *fcenæ committis, et* audes Perfonam *fcrmare* novam, *&c.* ————

in which he expreffes as ftrongly, as he can, what a daring attempt it would be to form a new character: but what a dull bufinefs muft the ftage have be-come by this time, had nothing been reprefented there but tirefome repetitions of the *carmen Iliacum*, nothing but a lumber-headed *Ajax*, a bawling *Ther-fites*, or an *Achilles*, who muft for ever have been juft the fame,

Impiger, iracundus, inexorabilis, acer !

cel the Ancients; through whoſe ſolemn
ſcenes, there ſtalks a certain ſtubborn heroic
kind of virtue, armed with a few principles
of juſtice and moral rectitude, and attended
by a ſet of ſtage decorums; but whoſe ſtern
countenance baniſhes all thoſe milder graces,
that * affect the heart, that force the invo-
luntary ſigh, and teach the reluctant tear to
flow?

* Neither let any one imagine, that their not affecting us is owing to the language, in which they
are wrote: let the moſt learned profeſſor in thoſe
languages tranſlate them into the beſt modern Engliſh, and the effect will ſtill be the ſame.

As they do not affect us much in the reading,
ſo is it difficult to imagine, how they could affect
people much more, in the way, in which they were
acted. They, who have ſeen ſome of our beſt ac-
treſſes, and have attended to the inimitable expreſ-
ſion in a *Garrick*'s features, will hardly ſee, how
theſe could be equalled in the old way of acting;
where men played women's parts, and all the characters were performed in maſks. Beſides, the
largeneſs of their theatres muſt have deſtroyed all
the ſoft and delicate inflexions of the voice. Neither
can one eaſily conceive, how their chanting and
muſical accompaniments could ſupply theſe defects.
Indeed it is but a poor opinion one can entertain of
their attainments in this art: from any thing I have
ever read or heard either of their muſic, or muſical
inſtruments, I ſhould conclude, that if all the muſic
in this Iſland, muſical inſtruments, and muſicians
too, were ſent in cargos, like the Jeſuits, to his
holineſs the Pope; excepting only Mr. *Parry* and
his welch harp; we ſhould have almoſt as much
muſic

flow? Thefe will in vain be fought for in the antient drama; where the tragedies have fcarce any other marks of being fuch, but a few αι αι, Φευ Φευ's occafionally difperfed about in them; and the actors in general are merely a fect of unfeeling bufkined philofophers; who deliver in a tedious unaffecting kind of dialogue their imperfect maxims to be commented upon by the Chorus; † whofe

bu-

mufic left, as *Rome* or *Athens* ever knew. I am not ignorant of the furprifing ftories, which are told concerning the power of antient mufic. But at the fame time I know, that thofe people are always moft apt to be furprifed, who are leaft acquainted with any matter. Nothing is fo ready to ftare and wonder itfelf, or endeavours fo much to make others ftare and wonder, as ignorance. Hence *Græcia mendax* had it's name, as much as for any other reafon; and it is probable, that Egypt deferved the title ftill better.

I am aware, that this ftricture upon old plays and the manner, in which they were acted, will lay me open to many cenfures; both for my want of tafte, and want of reverence. But,

—— *Clament* (which I would conftrue, " Let them cry out, as loud, as they pleafe,") *periiffe pudorem*
    Cuncti pene patres ; ea cum reprehendere coner
    Quæ gravis Æfopus, quæ doctus Rofcius egit !
Since I know the reafons of the outcry would be only,
    Vel quia nil rectum, nifi quod placuit fibi, ducunt;
    Vel quia turpe putant parere minoribus, et quæ
    Imberbi didicere, fenes perdenda fateri.

† *Ille regit dictis animos et pectora mulcet.*

business it is to prevent either their being moved themselves, or moving you; for which indeed there generally seems but little occasion for them to exert much care.

The most pity-moving character of any I remember among them, is that of *Electra*; but compare that, as described by either of the *Poets, with the gentle *Elfrida*; and you will soon perceive, how far beyond what the antients ever knew, the moderns have carried all the milder virtues of humanity, that delicacy of sentiment, that tenderness of disposition, and soft complacency, which are the peculiar characteristics of a refinement in manners †.

Hi-

---

* *Sophocles*, and *Euripides*.

† However trifling or superficial this rule, of forming a judgement of the manners of a people from their entertainments, may seem to some, it is certainly much better, than any, which depends on history: for an historian may be partial, may palliate and excuse; but the poet, who writes for the stage, whose avowed end is to please the people, will undoubtedly in forming his characters, copy, or at least, pay a principal regard to the manners of that people: and if we find him introducing into his scenes a set of actions, which hurt rather than move us, we may be sure, the age he wrote in, was barbarous in some degree, whatever fine names an historian may have honoured it with; just as we certainly know a late age was grossly superstitious, from the number of ghosts and apparitions, introduced into all the plays that were then wrote.

Hitherto I have only mentioned the Tragedians, but the Epic poets alſo have availed
themſelves of the ſame advantage: nor can
I in the leaſt doubt, but that a great part of
that univerſal homage, which is paid to *Homer*, *Virgil*, and *Milton*, is owing to the antiquity of their ſubjects. And if the laſt of
the three has really excelled the other two,
I ſuſpect it is in nothing ſo much, as in having gone beyond them in this article. •

If inſtead of *Man's firſt diſobedience*, &c.
Milton had ſung of *Their firſt diſobedience*,
who, by a paſſionate ſtruggle for liberty, had
well-nigh brought about the ſlavery both of
themſelves and their poſterity; (though a
ſubject this of a moſt intereſting nature to
us of this kingdom, and one, with which he
muſt have been moſt thoroughly acquainted,)
he would have found it extremely difficult,
with all his force of numbers, to have ſe-
cured himſelf from being placed upon the
ſame ſhelf with Prince *Arthur's* poet; and
might perhaps have ſtood there, as little
noticed.

Nay, the divine *Homer* himſelf, were he
to come to life again, with the very ſame
powers he had before; and attempt to ſing
the wars of *Germany* during the three laſt
campaigns;

campaigns, with all the noble exploits of *Frederic* and *Ferdinand* for his materials, would never be able to produce a work of equal eſtimation with the *Iliad*,

—— *Adeo ſanctum vetus omne!* ——

Though ſuch a paultry buſineſs, as the taking of *Troy*, would not have been a work of ten days to one of our modern armies; in which the hero *Achilles* would not, without much inſtruction, have military ſkill enough to rank as a ſubaltern.

But ten long years of ſiege ſome thouſand years ago, or a * war in heaven, (the very ſound of which, by the way, almoſt ſtaggers ſober reaſon, without an abſurd enumeration of particulars) ſets admiration on the wide gape, and with that on his ſide, let the poet raiſe what monſters he will, they all go glibly down,

Scyllamque Antiphatemque, et cum Cyclope Charybdin.——

It

* It would be extremely difficult to determine, whether the Deities of the Heathen poet, or the Angels of the Chriſtian, make the beſt warriors; though the latter have one manifeſt advantage over the former; I mean that of gunpowder, and a large train of artillery. ————

Surely a Chriſtian Poet could never have fallen into ſuch an abſurdity, had it not been through a ſtudious imitation of the Heathen!

It is amazing to think, what outrageous nonfenfe we are reconciled to, by this fingle charm of antiquity. All the trumpery of idle fables, and old ftories, which nothing, but being old, could fecure from being laughed at, is, when dreffed in this venerable garb, received with the moft profound deference, and fanctimonious regard.*

Next to the poets may be reckoned, as auxiliaries in the fame caufe, the whole body of declamers, of what denomination foever; from the public orator down to the private murmurer and complainer about debts and taxes; from him, who pours forth his eloquence in the fenate or the pulpit, to him, who, in

* Of this *Virgil* feems to have been well aware, when, intending to defcribe fome religious rites of his countrymen, things of a ticklifh nature to meddle with, he thought proper (if we may credit the ingenious interpretation of the fixth book of the *Æneid*, given us by the learned author of *The Divine Legation of Mofes*) to mafk his intention, not only for greater fecurity, but alfo for greater dignity, under the hallowed covering of a defcent into the regions below.

One trembles to think, how many marks of refemblance, to how many venerable affemblies, an ingenious critic, by the application of this rule, may hereafter difcover in *Milton*'s *Pandæmonium!* who can fay, that the poet in this, had not an eye to the famous meeting of Divines at *Weftminfter?*

in an humbler ſphere, contents himſelf with
haranguing the political circle of a coffee-
houſe, or a neigbouring club; who have all
made it their buſineſs to ſpeak as ill as poſſible of times preſent; having, perhaps, for
their encouragement, found it to be true,
that the poignancy of ſatyr was better ſuited
to the common palates of mankind, than
the inſipid flatneſs of panegyric; and that
we like, in general, much better to be
frightened and abuſed, than even to be praiſ-
ed and flattered.

As many however of this claſs betray ſuch
an unreaſonable malignancy in their cenſures, one is almoſt ready to conclude, that
they were born with a natural indiſpoſition
to be pleaſed.

Many more of them through prejudice,
diſappointment, or education, ſeem to have
acquired a certain habit of ſeeing things in
a wrong light, and repreſenting them ſo to
others.

And if to theſe we add the number of
ſuch, as without any kind of conviction, or
even examination at all about the matter,
fall into trite common-place harangues
againſt the vices of the times; merely becauſe it has been long the practice ſo to do,

and

and it is become eafy therefore to go on in the beaten track; we fhall not leave many behind, who deferve our notice.

There is indeed one fort of them, who are of much better quality, than any of the above defcribed; whofe account of things, though given with a much better intention, is yet as far from being true, as any of the others. I mean thofe zealoufly good men, who purpofely defcribe the wickednefs of mankind in as black colors, as they can, to make them ftart, if poffible, at the frightful picture; and who, in order to awaken their hearers to a vigorous profecution of virtuous meafures, endeavor to alarm them thoroughly, with the greatnefs of their danger in a contrary courfe: to do which more effectually, they are fometimes tempted to ftep afide from the exact limits of truth, and borrow a ftriking feature of vice from the regions of fancy.

Whether, or no, their fuccefs has been equal to their honeft intention, is no part of our inquiry: but admitting their own account of things to be true, it feems, as if it had not; for they fucceffively go on to defcribe the times, as growing worfe and worfe, notwithftanding their moft earneft endeavours to the contrary.

I do not mean, that therefore ſin ſhould be flattered; or that a wicked age ſhould have nothing, but "ſmooth things propheſied unto it:" though conſidering how ill the contrary method has ſucceeded, it might not perhaps be amiſs to try, what giving men a more comfortable proſpect would do : we always preſs forward with greater eagerneſs; and there is a certain uphill kind of labor in attaining to heights, from whence we are ſuppoſed to have fallen, which muſt needs move ſlowly on. But there is undoubtedly ſufficient reaſon, for the friends of virtue at all times to aim at inſpiring men with a lively ſenſe of their duty, and not to neglect any method, which may anſwer that good end.

All therefore, which I would be underſtood to mean by what I have ſaid above, is no more than this, that the character of an age ought not to be taken ſtrictly from ſuch intereſted accounts, as theſe; where there is ſome other end to be anſwered, beſides the mere diſcovery of truth.

To the cauſes already aſſigned, as likely to give riſe to the common miſtake, (and which are ſwelled, I am afraid, to a tedious number,) I will add but this one more, *the natural inclination of all mankind*, to aſ-
cribe

cribe their unhappinefs to any thing whatever, rather than to themfelves : if we refleĉt
then, how uneafy they are for ever making
themfelves in their prefent circumftances,
be they what they will, by their follies and
their vices; and yet how willing they are to
remove the blame of this from their own
doors; we need not be furprifed, if we find
them all fond of attributing the uneafinefs
they fuffer, more to the natural badnefs of
the times, in which they live, than to reafons, which might throw a refleĉtion on
their own conduĉt.

And from all thefe confiderations, taken
together, we may furely difcover abundant
room, whenever it firft happened, for the
opinion to obtain, " that prefent times fell
far fhort of the excellency of former days."
And when once an error has got ground, it
not only grows of itfelf, without either cul-
ture or care ; but it requires much both of
time and pains to root it out.

Having thus traced out the fources, from
which men have probably derived their
common notion, that the world has been
growing worfe and worfe continually; it may
be almoft argument enough to fhew it's
falfehood, juft to obferve, that had it been
true;

true, there muſt have been an end of the
world, and it's wickedneſs too, before this
time: it is ſuch a downhill road to ruin and
perdition, that had men entered upon it; had
they begun to decline in virtue and perfection, ſo early and ſo faſt, as theſe complaints
would make them; they muſt long e'er this
have reached the loweſt pitch of degeneracy;
and the bands by which ſociety is held together, had been all long ago looſened and
deſtroyed.

CHAP. IV.

Of the evil tendency of this opinion, and the mifchief they do, who encourage it.

THIS opinion however is not only falfe, but like moft others, which are fo, it is of a moft pernicious tendency to civil peace and focial happinefs: and they, who encourage it, cannot well do a worfe office to mankind.

This is no piece of refined modern policy, but was long ago difcovered by a great king and moral teacher; who has left us the following maxim; " Say not thou, what is the caufe, that the former days were better than thefe? for thou doft not inquire wifely concerning this." Which words I fhall beg leave to confider as a text to preach upon to the end of this chapter.*

The meaning then of this maxim may, firft of all, be conftrued thus, " Do not fet about inquiring into the caufe of a thing, which is not in itfelf true in fact." This would be to inquire unwifely indeed!

We

---

* I thought proper to declare this, that thofe of my readers, whofe ftomachs are too weak to bear any thing in the fermon way, may pafs it over.

We might, notwithſtanding, be thought perhaps to extend this meaning to ſuch a length, as however ſuitable it might be to our purpoſe, would ſcarce be agreeable to that wiſdom, for which the author of the precept was ſo highly and ſo juſtly celebrated, if we ſhould infer from it, that he intended abſolutely to prohibit all inquiry into this ſubject whatever, which ſhould be on the unfavorable ſide: — becauſe, if we are really convinced, that our preſent circumſtances fall far ſhort of the excellency of former times; (a caſe which may happen to a particular place, whilſt at the ſame time the general plan of improvement is ſtill carrying on in the world at large;) we ſurely not only may, but in prudence ſhould, endeavour to trace out the cauſe, from whence that former ſuperiority aroſe ; by which means we might perhaps both ſee, how we had gone off from that good principle ; and alſo be enabled to find out a method of returning into the right way again.

If then it be allowed, that the maxim is not ſo ſtrictly prohibitory; it might in the next place be made matter of diſpute, whether it was meant, as a piece of inſtruction to thoſe, who ſhould hereafter direct their inquiries

4   this

this way, to ufe the utmoſt caution and prudence; or, as a reproof to thoſe, who had already conducted themſelves in this buſineſs
by other principles; who had ſhewn an unreaſonable diſſatisfaction at the preſent order
of things, and from thence had proceeded to
haſty and petulant concluſions againſt it.

And farther, if we even confine the precept to the laſt mentioned ſenſe; it may ſtill
be doubted, whether it was levelled only
at the common diſcontentedneſs of mankind in general; or was pointed more immediately at ſome particular * perſon; who
might be famous, in *Solomon's* days, for having inſtituted a compariſon between thoſe
and former times, in favor of the latter.

But however doubtful theſe points may
be, it is clear beyond all doubt, that this
wiſe man intended to diſcourage all ſuch inquiries,

* I would beg leave to obſerve, that it is no proof
of the abſurdity of this ſuppoſition; that we, at this
diſtance of time, know nothing more concerning the
exiſtence of any ſuch perſon; becauſe it is much to be
queſtioned, whether, at the ſame diſtance of time
from the preſent, with all the advantages, which modern authors have from the invention of printing, it
will not be to the full as uncertain, that ever *we* had
ſuch an author amongſt *us*.

quiries, as could answer no other end, but to
furnish fresh matter of complaint to peevish
and froward minds; and increase the dissatis-
faction, which men are apt enough of themselves to conceive against the conditions, in
which they are placed : if he farther designed what he says, as a stricture upon some
particular Cenfor of the times, it certainly
was, because he knew him to be one of this
turn ; one, who *did not inquire wisely concerning this* ; but had taken up his facts, perhaps,
on flight evidence, and had been guided, even
in his reasoning upon these facts, more by
caprice than judgement ;— in short, one, who
had shewn his abilities to declame and rail at
what every one, as well as himself, could see
was amiss, rather than any penetration into
the caufe, from whence the evil sprung; or
skill in prescribing a remedy, by which it
might be cured.

And whenever a person sets about such inquiries as these, merely out of disguft at some
present disappointment, or to satisfy a sple-
netic disposition, which is ever fond of find-
ing fault; when, in consequence of this, his
representations are plainly drawn, more from
ill temper, or a desire to lash and expose the
age, than a fober inclination to reform it;
when

when he ſhews manifeſt ſymptoms of virulence, pique, and reſentment, things intirely
inconſiſtent with the character of a candid
inquirer; when he betrays either paſſion or
pride, things utterly unbecoming a moral
reformer; — the reproof of *Solomon* is ſtill
juſtly applicable to him, " Say not *thou*,what
is the cauſe that the former days were better
than theſe ? for *thou* doſt not inquire wiſely
concerning this". The moſt favorable con
ſtruction, that can be put upon ſuch a man's
attempts to depreciate the times, in which he
lives, (eſpecially, if he takes the advantage of
any diſheartening circumſtances to ſpread his
poiſon more ſucceſsfully;) is, that he is endeavouring to purchaſe an opinion of his
own ſuperior diſcernment, even at the expence of his honeſty ;* is charitably undertaking to undeceive others, who by ſome
miſtake are happy ; and is trying, as much
as in him lies, to diffuſe that chagrin and ill
humor, which mark his own gloomy brow,
into minds of a better turn, and more cheerful

---

* For, as the author of the late Eſtimate well expreſſes it, " To rail at the times at large, can ſerve
no good purpoſe ; and generally ariſeth from a want
of knowledge, or a want of honeſty." *Eſtimate*,p.15.

ful diſpoſition ; by which means, if he is of
conſequence enough to be attended to, (and
indeed, what is there, that bodes ill to mankind, but is thought of conſequence enough
to be attended to ? *) he does infinite miſchief
to the community, of which he is a member;
the ſtability and happineſs of which conſiſt
in nothing ſo much, as in being thought well
of by thoſe, who compoſe it.

* " Vice impatiently drinks in, and *applauds* his
hoarſe and boding voice, while like a *Raven*, he ſits
croaking univerſal death, *deſpair*, and annihilation
to the human kind." *Eſtimate*, p. 169.

CHAP.

CHAP. V.

In which some other opinions are considered.

BESIDES the opinion, already taken notice of, there are some others, which may seem to stand in our way ; and which therefore it may be proper to remove, before we attempt to proceed any farther.

To avoid then, in part, the abfurdity of fuppofing things to have been continually growing worfe and worfe, fome may fancy, that the world, like a day,* as it has had it's morning, muft alfo have it's evening : they may allow, that, for a time, it muft have been improving ; that the dawn could not pretend to vie with that blaze and fplendor, which fhould mark the mid-day height; but, this being once over, things would be upon the decline again ; till they were loft in end-lefs night.

Now, admitting this to be poffible, will they fay this imaginary *vertex* is already paft? if it be, where muft we look to find the æra, when that moft fingular event happened ?

Was

* The courfe of human affairs, having begun in the eaft, and travelled weftward, may be thought to give fome countenance to this opinion.

Was it at *Babylon*, or *Memphis*; at *Athens*, or at *Rome*, that worldly greatnefs attained this fancied fummit of perfection?—If it be not paft already, which the lofs men are at to point out clearly the time, when it happened, fhews fufficiently it is not; there is every appearance to prove, that the world is not yet near it, though nearer now, than ever it was before; and there is all the reafon, which analogy can afford, to affure us, that it will never pafs it; but will go on, from one degree of advancement to another, till it has reached the higheft point, for which it was defigned; when it will yield up it's inhabitants to other worlds, and greater blifs, than it could give them.*

Others,

* It might appear a whimfical conjecture, to fuppofe, that in our future exiftence we may poffibly pafs through all the different planets, both in this and other folar fyftems : yet, if we are to have bodies hereafter, and a local habitation, this might perhaps be made as plaufible an hypothefis, as many others, which have carried their heads full high in the literary world. What our Saviour fays, " That in his Father's houfe are many manfions", might with as little force be brought to confirm this, as many other texts of Scripture have been dragged from their original meaning to give evidence for fome theological whimfy. And, if we look into the internal conftitution of this great globe itfelf, which we inhabit,

Others, however feem to have thought, there was a certain † equality in human affairs, above or below which they never rofe much higher, or funk much lower ; but that all fublunary things, as if under the more immediate influence of that planet, from whence they have their name, were actuated by a kind of tide ; which, by turns, would occafion a flow, as it were, in fome places, and an

ebb

bit, we fhall fee many appearances, which might lead us to imagine, that it was a place of abode for other animals, before it was fitted up for our reception.

On fome fuch fuppofition, as the above, the Poet's Hell feems to have been built ;

Ay, but to die, and go we know not where, &c.

——— *The dilated Spirit*
To bathe in fiery floods ; or to refide
In thrilling regions of thick-ribbed ice!

† To this opinion may poffibly be referred the adage of *Solomon,* " That there is nothing new un- " der the Sun ; But the thing that hath been, it is " that which fhall be, and that which is done, is that " which fhall be done, &c". — And likewife what *Sophocles* fays in his Ajax;

Απανθ' ὁ μακρος κἀναριθμηῖ◎ χρον◎
Φυει τ' αδηλα κ̓ Φανεῖα κρυπῖεῖαι.——

There is a paffage too in *Tacitus* to the fame purpofe ;
" Nifi forte rebus cunctis ineft quidam velut *or-* " *bis,* ut quemadmodum temporum vices, ita mo- " rum vertantur."

ebb in others; each of which would be fol-
lowed again by it's reſpective ebb and flow,
in regular ſucceſſion.

And, in fact, ſomething very like this has
happened in the world. States and Empires
have had their riſe and fall; different places,
at different times, have been the envied ſeats
of learning, power, and greatneſs; and, in
their turns again, have become the contempt-
ible reſidence of ignorance, ſlavery, and
meanneſs. Temples, Porticos, and Towers,
the palaces of Princes, and the ſchools of
Philoſophers, have, in this ſtrange revolution,
been baſely converted into huts for peaſants,
and ſtalls for their cattle!

Theſe great and numerous inſtances of
the injurious effects of time, we may, we
muſt lament; the very dread of what may
hereafter happen to our own loved country,
will enforce a feeling, and compaſſionate regard for theſe vaſt overthrows of former
magnificence : and yet perhaps, they were
the neceſſary means of bringing *us* to that
towering height of fortune, to which we are
now raiſed. Providence might act in this
caſe, as we ſee the ſkilful huſbandman do;
who, when he has had as many crops from
one field, as the ſoil will yield, which now

by

by frequent tilling is worn out, turns his attention to fome other fpot; and breaks up frefher ground, in hopes of larger increafe, and a more ample return for his labor.

But however this may be, certain it is, that though deluges and earthquakes, the ravages of fire and fword, with other the eventful ftrokes of time, have delayed the progrefs of human things toward perfection, they have not intirely prevented it; earthly greatnefs, like the earth-born Giant, feems to have recovered frefh ftrength every time it has been thrown to the ground; and even after that long period, in which arts and fciences laid as it were dormant, they have awaked, as if refrefhed by this fleep, with new vigor.

Indeed from the moft thorough wrecks of time, there has always fomething ef-caped; if not as much, as we might wifh, at leaft enough to enable fucceeding ages to fet out on their inquiries, with greater ad-vantage, than *they* could poffibly have, *who* had every thing to invent anew : even a boat, or plank properly fhaped, efcaping, would eafily furnifh ideas to future projec-tors, which probably coft the firft inventor many a painful refearch.

And

And even from this ſeeming objection, I think, one might draw an almoſt undeniable argument in favor of modern improvements: ſince theſe deſtructions, which happened to former arts and learning, might be accounted for from natural cauſes; for, when all the learning of mankind was in one empire, in one country, and perhaps in one city, it might be eaſy for ſuch an event to happen, as would almoſt intirely deſtroy it. But in the diffuſed ſtate, which learning and arts are in at preſent, under the care and protection of ſeveral different governments, who are all jealous of maintaining their reſpective ſhare; it muſt be the hand of God alone, raiſed to inflict a general puniſhment for our ſins, that could bring about any thing like what happened before on events merely natural.

But if this be the caſe; if it be really true, that we are now in poſſeſſion of greater advantages, than God ever gave to men before; what ſhould the conſequence be on our part, but greater degrees of virtue to deſerve, and of diligence to improve them!

Λ

A NEW
ESTIMATE
OF
MANNERS and PRINCIPLES.

PART II.
Of the Knowledge of Mankind.

Alius error est, suspicio quædam et diffidentia, quæ nihil nunc posse inveniri autumat, quo mundus tamdiu carere potuit ; ac si illa objectio conveniret erga tempus, quâ Lucianus impetit Jovem, cæterosque ethnicorum Deos : "Miratur enim, cur tot olim genuerint liberos, nullos autem suo sæculo ? interrogatque jocans, ecquid septuagenarii jam essent, aut lege Pappiâ contra senum nuptias constricti ?" sic videntur homines subvereri, ne tempus effætum jam factum sit et ad generationem ineptum.   Lord BACON.

But for myself, (says the great Sir WALTER RALEIGH) *I shall never be persuaded, that God hath shut up all the light of Learning within the Lanthorn of Aristotle's brains; or, that it was ever said unto him, as unto Esdras,* Accendam in corde tuo Lucernam intellectus; *That God hath given invention but to the Heathen, and that they only invaded Nature, and found the strength and bottom thereof ; the same Nature having consumed all her store, and left nothing of price to after-ages.*

TO THE

SOCIETY

FOR ENCOURAGING

Arts, Manufactures, and Commerce,

This SECOND PART

Treating of ARTS and SCIENCES,

IS

Humbly offered,

As a mark of the Author's great respect.

————— *Nec* omnia *apud priores* meliora, *sed nostra quoque ætas* multa Laudis *et* Artium, *imitanda posteris reliquit.* TACIT.

PART II.

Of the Knowledge of Mankind.

CHAP. I.

A general view of what is propofed in the fecond part.

HAVING attempted to remove fome objections which feemed to ftand in my
way, and threatened to oppofe my conclu-
fion, I fhall now undertake a more direct
proof of the propofition, which I laid down
in the firft part; namely, " That all ages and
countries taken collectively, the world is, and
has been from the earlieft notice we have
of it, in a ftate of general improvement" ;
or, which is nearly the fame thing in o-
ther words, " That mankind at prefent is
wifer, happier, and *better* than it ever was
before."

This, it muft be owned, is a wide and
open field, and the paths acrofs it are but
faintly marked ; the herd has gone another
way ; people hitherto have paid fuch a deference to venerable antiquity, as to imagine,

D   that

that the longer ago men lived, they were for that reaſon, and in that proportion, wiſer and better; having ſeemingly made this miſtake amongſt others, that by hearing the terms, *ancient* and *old*, applied to former times, they have really been led to ſuppoſe the world older, and therefore wiſer heretofore, than it is now: whereas in fact, thoſe* early times were the youthful days of the world; which is now, if not in it's old age, at leaſt in a much more advanced ſtage, than it was then; and conſequently has a ſtronger claim to that wiſdom, which greater age gives, than ever it had before.

With this appearance then on my ſide, eſpecially as knowledge ſeems to be the grand principle, on which all other improvements depend, I will begin with endeavoring to ſhew, that men are wiſer now, than they formerly were; or, that *ſcience* and the *arts of life* are at preſent in a ſtate of much higher perfection, than they ever were, at any former period.

It

---

* Sane, ut verum dicamus, *Antiquitas ſæculi Juventus mundi.* Noſtra profecto ſunt antiqua tempora, cum mundus jam ſenuerit, non ea quæ computantur ordine retrogrado initium ſumendo a ſæculo noſtro. Lord *Bacon.*

It can hardly be neceſſary, one ſhould think, to explain, what one means by ſuch common terms, as *ſcience* and the *arts of life:* leſt however any miſtake ſhould be made; I mean, by *ſcience,* all that knowledge, which mankind are poſſeſſed of, by what means ſoever acquired, or of whatever ſort it be; and, by the *arts of life,* I underſtand the practical production of ſcience into uſe, comprehending all thoſe various inventions, which contribute, in any degree, to ſupply men either with neceſſaries, conveniencies, elegancies, or even amuſements.

To be accurate, one ſhould perhaps make theſe two the ſubjects of two diſtinct conſiderations; it being poſſible, that the arts of life may flouriſh in ſome degree, where ſcience languiſhes; as luxury, which is evidently a friend to the one, may be thought by ſome an enemy to the other; ſo that the ſame concluſion might not be juſt, when extended to them both indiſcriminately: but they have generally grown up together in ſuch cloſe connexion, that there is little room left for the ſuſpicion of their ever being parted; and therefore it ſeems needleſs to conſider them aſunder: beſides, much accuracy is not to be expected in

ſuch

such a loose way of estimating things, as I am pursuing; in which I aim at nothing more, than just to touch upon the surface of such matters, as lie open to view, and seem to invite the eye; while I leave it to the more discerning and judicious to pry, with more exactness, into less obvious distinctions.

CHAP.

CHAP. II.

'A proof, that Arts and Sciences muſt have been improving, drawn from the nature of the thing.

THAT arts and ſciences have been, upon the whole, in an improving ſtate, from the beginning of the world to this time, is, ſtrictly, to be proved only by the authority of hiſtory, or matter of fact, as it ſtands related there. Yet ſuch a degree of probability ariſes from the very nature of the thing, as may make it ſeem unneceſſary to attempt a direct and formal proof.

For if, as ſacred hiſtory informs us, mankind derived it's being from two original parents; how neceſſarily muſt theſe two, ignorant and unſkilled at firſt, unleſs they were to live by mere inſtinct only, make daily advances in ſome new diſcoveries, either of what was needful, or convenient for them! allowing them to have received, from their Maker, ſome * ſlight information about

* Some of the learned (as *Heidegger* and *Delany*) have taken a great deal of pains, to ſhew, that *Adam* had very numerous revelations made to him : I do not mean at all to interfere with their ſtudious labors ; but allowing him to have received all the information, they pretend he did, if he was made a rational creature, all, that I can contend for, will be equally true.

D 3

bout what was fit for them to eat, what
they ſhould do, or what avoid; would their
own experience, think ye, make no addition
to theſe firſt impreſſions, this ſo ſcanty fund
of knowledge? would not they find towards the cloſe of life, that they knew
much more, than they did at the beginning of it? would they not perceive, that
had they known things at firſt, as well as
they did then, they could have got through
life more comfortably, than they had done?
and would not they treaſure up theſe docu-
ments of experience, as uſeful leſſons to their
children? Theſe queſtions are ſo very clear,
that they contain their anſwers. Their
children then, even ſuppoſing them not to
make all the uſe of inſtruction, which they
might, would certainly, by this means, ſet
out in the world with much greater advantages, than their parents had done: and in
a ſucceſſion of generations, ſuppoſing the
natural abilities of mankind to be the ſame,
this muſt continue for ever to be the caſe.

I do not mean, by this, to encourage
every raw and unfledged upſtart, with an
overweening opinion of his own towering
genius, to think himſelf wiſer than his
teachers; or of more underſtanding than the

4   aged.

aged. It is, no doubt, a mark of duty to believe our parents and inſtructors wiſer, than
ourſelves; (which, if the principles laid down
above be true, they muſt be;) and it would
be well, if we would liſten to their wiſdom
more, than we uſually do. But ſurely to
ſuppoſe, that, with all our health and
ſtrength about us, we can go no farther,
than their kindneſs has conducted us, can
be the ſign of nothing, but mere ſloth or
ſhallow conceit.

Yet this fondneſs, either for ſtaying
where we are, or at leaſt, going on only
in the * old way; or the ſame notion
in other words, an over-readineſs to fancy
it impoſſible to carry the land-marks of
know-

* Certe conſilium Prophetæ vera in hac re nor-
ma eſt, " State ſuper *vias antiquas*, et videte quæ-
nam ſit via recta et bona, & ambulate in eâ." Antiquitas eam meretur reverentiam, ut homines ali-
quamdiu gradum ſiſtere, et ſupra eam ſtare debeant,
atque undequaque circumſpicere, quæ ſit via op-
tima : quum autem de viâ bene conſtiterit, tunc
demum non reſtitendum, ſed alacriter progredien-
dum. Lord *Bacon* de Aug. Scient.

But ſurely, if we can perceive none of the old
ways to be right and good, or that are likely to
lead us to a concluſion of our preſent purpoſe; we
are at liberty to chooſe one of our own; or we can
never arrive at any new diſcovery.

knowledge farther, than where our fathers had fixed them, aided by the abfurd ridicule, which is ufually thrown upon all new attempts by thofe felf-fatisfied men, who are laudably determined to take things, as they find them; has been one grand hinderance, that has occafioned the flow movement of human inventions towards perfection. *

But leaving this reflexion, let us fuppofe mankind to be now fo far increafed by degrees, as to have become, at firft, too numerous for one family; and afterwards, for one country to contain. Neceffity, in this cafe, would oblige the too populous commonweal to difcharge itfelf of a part of it's cumbrous weight, and to fend away fome of it's fuperfluous inhabitants; who muft go in fearch

of

---

* Sapientiam fibi adimunt, qui fine ullo judicio inventa majorum probant, & ab aliis pecudum more ducuntur. *Lact.* de Orig. Erroris. l. 2. c. 8. "By the advantage of which floth and dulnefs, (as Sir *Walter Raleigh* quaintly, but ftrongly, expreffes it) ignorance is now become fo powerful a tyrant, as it hath fet true Philofophy, Phyfic and Divinity in a pillory; and written over the firft, CONTRA NEGANTEM PRINCIPIA; over the fecond, VIRTUS SPECIFICA; and over the third, ECCLESIA ROMANA."

of new habitations; in places, which before were uninhabited; in climates too, which differed much, from that they left, in foil, fruits, and temperature. Thefe new adventurers then, to make their fubfiftance eafy and comfortable, muft, befides the principles they brought from home with them, fet themfelves with all diligence, to find out and learn many other things, both ufeful and neceffary to be known. And this again would give rife to feveral new and valuable difcoveries. *

If we fuppofe, laftly, thefe feparate communities to be arrived at the higheft degree of perfection, which, independently of each other, they were capable of attaining; how vaftly would they all be improved by a mutual intercourfe with each other; and that in proportion to the eafe, and frequency of this intercourfe? what a number of things would be found in ufe among one people, that had never been thought of by the others; which yet might be introduced into their practice, with the greateft fuccefs?

Who-

---

* According to the old prophecy, " Men fhall go to and fro' upon the earth, and knowledge fhall be increafed."

Whoever conſiders, how much the art of navigation, the grand means of conveyance from one country to another, has lately been improved by the invention of the compaſs; and in conſequence of this, how much commerce has been extended; (whoſe intereſt it is to be acquainted, as much as poſſible, with the ways and manners of different people, whoſe buſineſs it is to ſupply the wants of one nation with the ſuperfluities of another, nay, whoſe ſtudy it is even to make ſuperfluities;) will eaſily ſee and allow, how much the advantages, which modern times have derived from this intercourſe, muſt exceed any, which could be obtained from it heretofore.

If any one thinks, that ſciences have not reaped the ſame benefit by this means, which arts have; — it muſt be merely, becauſe he looks upon ſcience to be built on different foundations, from thoſe of nature and experience; for otherwiſe, the improvements of them both muſt have been nearly equal.

CHAP.

CHAP. III.

The same propofition proved from a confideration of the places, where Arts have flourifhed.

THE Eaft, however well fuited it was for the firft race of mankind to make their appearance in, (as by it's genial warmth there would be a kind of fpontaneous produétion of fruits for their fubfiftence;) or however well it might be calculated for the fpeedy difperfion of mankind, (as it confifted chiefly of fruitful vales too narrow for an increafing multitude to dwell in, and difjoined from each other by large extenfive deferts;) it muft be, for the fame reafons, ill adapted to any confiderable improvements. The fame heat, which was favorable to the fruits of the earth, would be extremely injurious to the ftrength of the body, which would become languid and averfe to labor, the chief finew of all art and induftry. That large extent of continent too, with fuch vaft deferts in it, would render all trade and commerce extremely hazardous, and inconvenient; by which means, the arts would be deprived of their principal fupport and encouragement.

Greece.

Greece and *Italy* partook, in some respects, though in a less degree, of the inconveniencies of the East; and therefore, though their advancements in art were carried, considerably beyond the narrow bounds of their eastern predecessors; they must fall far short of what we, their more western, or rather more northern successors, have arrived at. The distinction which * *Tully* makes between the *Ligurians* and those of *Campania*, holds good, in some degree, between the *Italians* in general, and us of this island. They, born under a better sun, had little incitement to improvements, except from luxury or pleasure; which will never furnish such a goading spur to industry, as want can do: we, though we cannot, with reason, complain of nature's sparingness towards us, are placed in such a situation, as makes it necessary to earn her favors

---

* Speaking of the effect, which places have upon the manners of their inhabitants, he has the following words : " Non ingenerantur hominibus mores tam a stripe generis, ac seminis, quam ex iis rebus, quæ ab ipsâ naturâ loci, et vitæ consuetudine suppeditantur &c. *Ligures*, montani, duri atque agrestes. Docuit ager ipse nihil ferendo, nisi multâ culturâ, et magno labore quæsitum. *Campani*, semper superbi bonitate agrorum, et magnitudine fructuum, urbis salubritate, descriptione, pulchritudine. — Ex hac copia — arrogantia et luxuries." *De Leg. Agrar.*

favors, by a ftudious application of our own endeavors.

And, if there be * any truth in the old proverb, "That neceffity is the mother of invention," the moft numerous productions of art, are always to be expected in thofe places, where the defects of nature are the greateft.† The ftroller's motto, " vivitur ingenio," can never be fo true, as where men muft live by their wits, to live at all. In fhort, what could make a *Dutchman* ingenious but neceffity, and what but ingenuity could make fuch a marfh, as they live in, not only a habitable country; but one, which a few years ago,

could

---

* The number of my brother Authors, the refpectable inhabitants of Grub-ftreet, who write plainly from neceffity, and yet fhew no great marks of invention; may incline fome perhaps to think, that the proverb is not true in every inftance. And though I profefs not to write through neceffity, yet it may be well, if I myfelf efcape cenfure here.

† It will be found too to be in general true, that, where arts are moft numerous, (fuch is the friendly affiftance which they mutually lend each other!) there alfo they will be in the greateft perfection; fome few particulars only excepted, which owe the excellence they are brought to, to fome extraordinary circumftance, fuch as embalming amongft the *Egyptians*, fhooting with bows and arrows amongft the *Indians*, &c.

could vie with the greateſt and proudeſt. ſtate in *Europe?*

However, though neceſſity be the ſtrongeſt motive to put men upon the firſt trials of their ſkill, yet this end is ſoon ſatisfied; and the arts require a better pay-maſter, and much higher encouragement, than it can give, to ſhew themſelves in any great degree of perfection. It will follow from hence, that of all places arts muſt flouriſh moſt in thoſe, where nature has been rather ſparing in her choiceſt gifts ; and yet the genius and riches of the inhabitants incline them much to luxury and pleaſure.

If the ſituation of ſuch a place ſhould, moreover, afford opportunity for an extenſive commerce ; and the quantity of what are called ſtaple commodities ſhould farther make this commerce an advantageous one ; (ſo that even in acquiring elegancies men ac-quire freſh opulence, the means of getting more ;) here it is, that arts muſt naturally attain to the higheſt ſummit of improve-ment.

CHAP.

CHAP. IV.

*Of the evidence which hiftory gives to the above
particulars.*

TO the above, which may be called natural arguments in favor of modern
excellency, the teftimony of all hiftory, if we
follow it's guidance through the different
places, where the moft eminent of mankind
have had fucceffively their abode, will perfectly agree.

I am not going to collect materials for a
hiftory of arts and fciences; (though it
were much to be wifhed, that fuch a work
was undertaken by an able hand!) but perhaps the following general fketch, in which
no more is attempted, than barely to mark
a few outlines, may be thought no unfair re-
prefentation of the antient ftate of things.

In the Eaft, where the dawn firft arofe,
men lived, as it were, under a fort of twi-
light; which partook in a great degree of
that darknefs, which had preceded it. Their
knowledge muft have been as imperfect, as
the accounts we have of it can be fuppofed
to be: according to thefe, it confifted chiefly
of a few moral apologues, where the fhadow
was

was much larger, than the ſubſtance; a ſet of looſe ſcattered maxims of life; and ſome accidental diſcoveries in the properties of plants and herbs: Theſe, together with a very ſmall number of trifling obſervations on the heavens, conſtituting a ſhort rude ſyſtem of aſtronomy, or rather aſtrology, which aided, and in it's turn was aided by, their ſuperſtition, ſeem to make the ſum, if ſuch is to be called knowledge, of what the eaſtern ſages knew.

Their religion was ſuch, as their paſtoral life might eaſily be ſuppoſed to throw in their way; by their frequent contemplations on the heavens they might be led firſt to admire and wonder at, and from thence to revere and worſhip, what they ſaw moſt ſtriking there, the ſun, the moon, and the ſtars; which they might alſo perceive were of much benefit to them, by affording light and heat. And they were probably di-rected in the choice of what they ſhould offer to theſe objects of their worſhip, either to gain their favor, or avert their anger, by reflecting on what would be moſt agreeable to themſelves, in the ſame circumſtances.

Their civil government was plainly ſuited only to keep in awe beaſts of prey; ſuch as

man-

mankind could never have fubmitted to, but through ignorance, or neceffity. Whether parental authority ftept into the feat of empire, and arrogated to itfelf fupreme command; or whether the fears of the herd led them to feek protection under the conduct of fome one of greater ftrength, or cunning than the reft, might perhaps be difficult to determine. But certain it is, the firft fpecimens of human government do little credit to their origin: there was the moft abject flavery on the one hand, and the moft abfolute tyranny on the other, that imagination can well form.

The luxury of the eaftern emperors, as they became great, it muft be owned, gave confiderable encouragement for the arts to fhew themfelves; but they were hindered from attaining to any great degree of perfection by the narrownefs of their commerce; which extending no farther, than to countries of nearly the fame produce with their own, and confined to a few articles, fuch as corn, gems, and fpicery, afforded fmall variety for genius to exercife itfelf upon.

It muft be obferved here, that I except out of my account God's peculiar people, the people of *Ifrael*, together with the religion,

E ftatutes,

ſtatutes, and ordinances, which he gave them; theſe being of divine inſtitution, are not ſubject to thoſe general laws, by which the common courſe of things is regulated.

Egypt too and it's learning, is a ſubject, which I would willingly paſs over, not as fearing, it will make againſt me; but, (if it may be conſiſtent with the dignity of an author to own himſelf ignorant of any thing, that falls in his way,) becauſe I really know very little of the matter. Happy in what they poſſeſſed, like the modern *Chineſe*, they ſeem to have been little ſollicitous about getting any thing, their neighbours had; but extremely ſo in preventing others from having any intercourſe at all with them. Hence the Difficulty of ſaying, what they knew, or did not know. If any one however has a deſire of being better acquainted with them, he need only read the *Divine Legation of Moſes*; the author of which incomparable performance is, like the perſon he treats of, *learned in all the wiſdom of the Egyptians*; to ſuch a degree, that he can tell us exactly the time and occaſion, when they firſt began to write *running hand !*

In the mean time it ſeems clear to me, that their affectation of ſo much myſtery,

4   and

and fecrecy, was but, in general, a cover for their ignorance. True knowledge deals not in myftery, nor does it feek to be hid. Their deifying too the authors of ufeful difcoveries fhews fufficiently, that things were near their beginning amongft them. If, befides this, it be true, that *Grecian* learning was built upon their's.; we may well conclude, that the foundation was not higher, than the edifice.*

If we pafs from hence into *Greece*; we fhall find, that they gave a fhape and coloring to thofe outlines of knowledge, which their eaftern predeceffors had left them: to thofe rude and uncouth forms of letters, which they received from them, they added fubftance and finews, and formed a fmooth and moft harmonious language; with which they wrought wonders in the provinces of poetry and eloquence, pufhed on, as they were,

by

---

* Primi per figuras animalium Ægyptii fenfus mentis effingebant; et antiquiffima monimenta humanæ memoriæ impreffa faxis cernuntur; et literarum femet inventores perhibent. Inde Phœnicas, quia mari præpollebant, intuliffe Græciæ, gloriamque adeptos; tanquam repererint quæ acceperant. Quippe fama eft Cadmum claffe Phœnicum vectum, rudibus adhuc Græcorum populis artis ejus auctorem fuiffe, &c. TACIT. Annal.

by the hopes of living in the memories of
mankind after death; the only ſpecies of immortality, of which they had any ſteady
apprehenſion.

The looſe and unconnected maxims of
former wiſdom, they wrought into fine ſy-
ſtems of phyſics, ethics, and politics. They
refined their manners and extended their
commerce; which however, like their ſhips,
durſt not venture, even yet, far from the
ſhores, or launch into the deep.

But though other things, and morality
amongſt the reſt, received conſiderable improvements here; yet religion ſtill lay in the
ſame imperfect ſtate, it had been in, with
only this addition, that the catalogue of deities was enlarged; every virtue and every
vice having been taken into the liſt of
gods, and goddeſſes. Which practice is
however not ſo abſurd, as it ſounds. Till
men could arrive at juſt notions of the
unity, omnipotence, and omnipreſence, of
the true God; what properer method could
be thought of to keep them in awe, than to
inſpire them with a belief, that there was a
particular Deity, who preſided over every
thing, they had to do with; over every
action, thought, and motion of their will;

                                        to

to whom fuch or fuch behaviour would either be agreeable, or odious?

But whatever the improvements of *Greece* were, their knowledge was drawn more from the fchools, than common life; and confequently was much better fitted for difputes in the one, than for ufe in the other; was in fhort much more fuited to the concealment of error, than the difcovery of truth. The effect, it has had, has been accordingly, juft fuch, as might be expected. Whilft men were content to follow each other in the fame narrow path, they neither did, nor could, make any new difcoveries: all they could do, was merely to wrangle and difpute, by dint of fyllogifm, in defence of their common error. And it has coft the world more trouble to get rid of miftakes, thus entailed upon it by authority, than it has met with from all the other ftoppages, in the way to true fcience, whatfoever.

If we look into the writings of their moft eminent philofophers, we fhall find, that *Ariftotle*, inftead of following Nature, endeavored, by every ftratagem, to catch her in the fubtle nets of his logic, and to lead her after him in a ftring of predicaments: as

well

well might the ſpider have attempted to
bind the brindled lion in her cobweb.

It may be ſaid, he did not draw his confined notions from the academic ſchool; and
that *Plato* had better deſigns and more enlarged views: but if he had, it was a pity
he ſhould go into a wood in ſearch of truth,
inter ſylvas quærere verum; as he ſeems by
that means to have loſt both himſelf, and
all who came after him, in endleſs intricacies.
Had he choſe the more open country for
his proſpect, he might perhaps have had a
clearer view of thoſe abſtract forms and
ideas, which in the other ſituation puzzled
him ſo much: but that vapor and condenſed
air, which is apt to ſettle about trees and
groves, ſpoiled all, and rendered every thing
confuſed.

If theſe two great maſters of *Grecian* wiſdom excelled in any thing, it was in their
rules about government; but even theſe, (ex-
cluſive of the ideal part of them, which was
contrived only for *Utopia*,) were calculated,
more for *Greece*, than for the world at large.
Indeed *Greece* was the world then, and it's
ſeparate ſtates the different and reſpective
nations of it. How then ſhall we compare
the

the ftate of things, which obtained at that
time, to the prefent ? when that, which was
the whole world *then*, is *now* but one of the
meaneft and moft abject provinces, it con-
tains ?

Rome, the next feat of human grandeur,
made fmall advances, beyond what *Greece*
had done, except in extent of empire; a nation of warriors and patriots, full of con-
queft and the honor of arms, were attentive
to little elfe, except what immediately pro-
moted their favorite project, and great ambition of univerfal empire. And it was not,
till they had well nigh effected this grand
purpofe, that the arts gained any confiderable attention among them. Though, when
they did bend their thoughts this way, it
muft be owned, they made a moft furprifing
progrefs; they even outdid their mafters in
many inftances, and perhaps equalled them
in all; particularly in ethics, didactic and
fatiric poetry, they feem to have gone far
beyond the *Greeks*; *Tully*'s offices, *Horace*'s
epiftles and fatires, with thofe of *Juvenal*
and *Perfius*, ftanding almoft without a rival
to vie with them. And indeed their knowledge of all kinds appears to have been
much more accurate and defined, than that

of

of the *Greeks*. Their hiſtory has leſs of fable, and more of common life in it; and even their poetry has leſs of what has been ſince called romance, and more good ſenſe in it, than that of the others.

But the age of learning was extremely ſhort at *Rome*; no ſooner had it attained to any thing like maturity, than it fell, almoſt at once, into mere dotage; in which ſickly ſtate it languiſhed a few years; and then ſunk to nothing. It was not long, after arts and ſciences began to grow reſpectable here, that, the conſtitution being changed, and the ſeat of empire removed from it's native ſoil to a country, where it never throve, the vaſt fabric of *Roman* greatneſs fell to pieces, even by it's own * weight, as it were; and opened a paſſage for the inroads of thoſe horrid barbarians, who, being bred in poverty and ignorance, were better ſuited to mortify, and take a more ample revenge of thoſe haughty lords, who had long affected to be

maſters

---

* *Livy* ſays of it, before the event happened, "Ab "exiguis profecta initiis, eo creverat, ut jam *magni-* *tudine laboret ſua*." And farther adds, that he ſuppoſes his readers will haſten on "ad hæc nova quibus "jampridem *prævalentis* populi *vires ſe ipſe confi-* "ciunt."

mafters of the whole world; every monument of whofe pride now felt their favage hands.

The cloud of darknefs, which after this event, fo fatal to letters, overfpread the face of all human affairs, makes a moft dreadful void in the hiftory of fcience: though it was but the natural confequence of one nation's arrogating to itfelf fupreme dominion; which is no otherwife to be acquired, or maintained by thofe, who attempt it, than by carefully keeping to themfelves all learning, riches, and means of power from the reft of mankind, who are to be their flaves; and confequently they and learning muft fall together. This, it is to be hoped, will never again be the cafe; it cannot, at leaft, happen by the fame means, fo long as there are rival nations, jealous of each other's greatnefs, and whofe intereft it is, and is known to be, to maintain, what is called, a balance of power.

From this cloud mankind, fome years ago, happily emerged; and have recovered enough of antient learning, if not to fatisfy their curiofity, at leaft to inform them of almoft every thing material, that was known in the world before. The fpace included between

this

this æra and the preſent, is what in general I mean by modern times, when they are mentioned with reference to former ages; but it is equally true, that we have been improving from that time to this.

What compariſon then ſhall we inſtitute between antient knowledge and modern acquiſitions, when the whole ſum of the former makes but as it were the baſis, on which the latter are built? We can eaſily make all, that men formerly knew, our own; and then, without being tired with any previous ſearch, with all our vigor freſh about us, can from thence ſet out on new diſcoveries; which we are ſtill more likely to attain to, becauſe we can calmly look down from our eminence, and ſee where they, who went before us, were miſled and loſt their way; can correct their miſtakes, avoid their errors, and mark out, and purſue, with leſs embarraſsment, the direct road, which leads to truth.

CHAP. V.

A general comparison between ancient and modern learning.

IT is not to be fuppofed however, that I mean to affert every thing to have been error and miftake in thefe our fchoolmafters. I would not be fufpected of being capable of looking, with indifference, at thofe ftupendous inftances of former greatnefs, *Rome* and *Athens*. It is impoffible to furvey them without perceiving many circumftances, which ftrike the mind with awful admiration.

What * fuperftition to their gods, or adulation to their heroes vanity, led them to excel in, they carried to an amazing height of perfection. It is from hence we fee and own

---

* Perhaps a fimilar fuperftition in modern *Rome*, the adoration paid to the fhrines and pictures of faints, &c. may be as ftrong a reafon, as any other, why the *Italians* have continued fo long to excel in the arts of fculpture and painting. We know in fact, that amongft ourfelves fome of the nobleft fpecimens of architecture, we have to boaft of, were the works of *Gothic* ignorance, ftirred up by zeal and devotion, at a time, when it cannot be faid, the arts were in any degree of perfection, equal to the prefent.

own their ſuperior excellence in architecture, ſtatuary, and their appendant arts. But
they ſeem to have employed their genius
and induſtry, chiefly in ſome of the inferior
parts of ſcience ; and appear to have been
principally buſied; to have ſpent moſt of
their time and attention, in ornamenting
the inlets and gates of knowledge; as if
conſcious, it was not permitted to their un-
hallowed feet to enter into her temple.
Their goddeſs wore a *veil, and they either
durſt not, or did not, attempt to pull it off.
They knew ſcarce any thing, as we do. They
never ſearched into the hidden ſources of
ſcience. Their knowledge like the *Nile* was
divided into different channels, but they
knew nothing of it's head. They wrote laws;
but they underſtood nothing of the *ſpirit of
laws*. They reaſoned, but they were intirely
unacquainted with *the powers of the mind, or
how it acquired it's ideas*. They ſaw matter,
and they ſaw motion ; but they were quite
ignorant of the *nature* of the one, and of
the *laws*, by which the other was governed.
Their knowledge, in ſhort, was drawn rather

* *Velum meum revelavit nemo.*
Part of an old inſcription in an *Egyptian* temple of
Minerva.

ther from their own brain, than from nature. They trufted more to fancy, than to
facts : and, like thofe ingenious architects,
who begin their building from the roof,
they framed curious hypothefes, which had
no foundation to fupport them. Whereas
we, leaving the airy flights of imagination,
have taken the furer, though more humble
path of fober reafon and chaftized reflexion;
and ground our deductions on correct experiments, and accurate obfervation. Their
knowledge extended only to a few particulars; we know fomewhat of almoft every
thing, that can be known, the boundaries
of learning having been as much enlarged
by late difcoveries, as thofe of the habitable
globe have been by the addition of a new
world. The powers of mechanifm, and o-
ther parts of ufeful fcience have been carried to fuch perfection, as former times
could never have conceived poffible; to fuch
indeed, as the prefent may hardly efteem cre-
dible. To enumerate particulars is impoffible; the very catalogue and mere index of
our improvements would fill as many volumes, as heretofore contained all the knowledge, which mankind were poffeffed of.

CHAP.

CHAP. VI.

Some particulars, which are likely to be disputed.

NOtwithstanding the above general comparison turns out so favorable to present times; there are some, to whose narrow minds one particular art or science seems to include all excellence; and who, on that account, will still give the preference to former days.

It is for this reason the man of classic learning, who fancies, that all knowledge, of any worth, is confined to *grammar*, *rhetoric*, and *poetry*, will sigh, that his lot of life was not cast in the *Augustan* age. The *man of war* will wish, he had seen the dispositions of *Cæsar*, or of *Hannibal!* the devout and serious *Christian*, with a better heart, though not much better reason, will carry back his desire of having lived nearer to that memorable æra, when the Son of God, by coming into the world, enlightened and improved mankind.

Look into these respective ages, and you will find men wishing, in the same manner, to have lived farther back still; which shews of itself the wish to be absurd.

But

But let us examine, in their order, a little more narrowly into thefe feveral particulars, and bring their merits to a nearer view. *

* It may perhaps be faid, that I might have carried this chapter to a much greater length, by inferting many other particulars, which are as likely to be difputed with me, as the above. —— Indeed I believe, I might have made the chapter endlefs by that means; fo many, and fuch ftrenuous advocates have the ancients to defend their caufe in every inftance! a principal reafon of which may poffibly be this; boys are early flogged into a high opinion of their worth and excellence; and they cannot eafily bring themfelves to think afterwards, that all the harfh treatment, which they fuffered, on this account, from the *plagofus Orbilius*, who had the ordering of their youth, was for any thing lefs, than matters of the higheft importance: on the contrary, having at length, by labour and application, acquired a competent fkill in Greek and Latin, they are apt to imagine, they have attained the very fummit of human learning; and look down from thence on the other parts of it, as low and groveling. To this pride of theirs, we may add a love of eafe, which renders them unwilling to enter upon any new branch of knowledge, where all the drudgery of firft principles muft again be undertaken; efpecially, as they find their vanity fufficiently flattered already, by being looked upon in the eye of the world, as *polite fcholars*. If fome of our beft Englifh authors had the fanction given them of being taught at fchool; this attachment to antiquity, merely as fuch, would gradually wear off; boys would learn fenfe as well as found; and our language, in time, receive the improvements, of which it is capable.

CHAP.

C H A P. VII.

Of language, and those parts of science, which depend more immediately upon it, such as rhetoric, poetry, &c.

PLEASED with having learned to talk, the ancients took vast pains to shew the acquisition, they had made; hence the many bawbles of grammar, rhetoric, and poetry, to be found amongst them. But what are these more, than mere toys and rattles, well enough suited indeed to the infancy of the world, but which it's manly and more philosophic age must needs hold in low estimation?

All pretensions then to superior excellence, in these instances, might be given up on the side of the moderns, without interfering at all with the plan, which I have hitherto been advancing: since, though science in general be like a river, and increases the farther it is removed from the small springs, which gave rise to it; yet some parts of it resemble rather lakes or standing ponds, formed occasionally perhaps from the overflowings of the other, but which in return contribute nothing to it's enlargement;

ment; fo far from that, being incapable of increafe themfelves, beyond a certain pitch, they may accidentally be dried up, without affecting in the leaft degree the courfe of the other, which ftill runs on as before,

— " *Virefque acquirit eundo.*"

In fact, whatever depends upon experiment and obfervation, (which all the nobler and more ufeful parts of knowledge do) is capable of continual improvement. But eloquence and poetry, as foon as the language of a people is at all formed, may be as complete in a fingle age, as the experience of a thoufand could make them. Nay, early times have fome manifeft advantages in this refpect: their language muft neceffarily abound moft in metaphors and allufions, which are the great ornaments of eloquence and poetry: the fimplicity too of men's manners, at fuch times gives a boldnefs and freedom to their fentiments, which will hereafter be expreffed with more caution and diffidence. Even their knowing no better raifes a * confidence,

* We have an inftance of this kind of affurance given us by *Suetonius.* "Germanorum legatis in or-
" cheftra federe permifit (*Claudius*) *fimplicitate* eo-
" rum & *fiducia* motus, quod in popularia deducti,
" quum animadvertiffent Parthos & Armenios fe-
" dentes in fenatu ad eadem loca fponte tranfierunt."

And

fidence, and an honeſt aſſurance in them, which add a wonderful force and energy to what they ſay. And it is highly probable, that the *Indian* chiefs, who now figure it ſo much in oratory before the aſſemblies of our colonies, will grow leſs eloquent, though not leſs learned, as they become more civilized, and leave off throwing down their belts of wampum, at the cloſe of their periods.

A particular reaſon too might be aſſigned, why the *Greeks* and *Romans*, when their manners became more refined, ſhould excel *us* in theſe inſtances. *They* had * error to deck out; *we*, truth: the former of which is a much finer ſubject for fiction and flowing language, than the latter. The tinſel and paint, which add charms to the harlot,

would

And perhaps the ſpeech given to our countryman *Caractacus* by *Tacitus*, which ſeems drawn on purpoſe to ſuit a ſimplicity of manners, is the fineſt piece of oratory, that ever was included in ſo ſmall a quantity of words.

* So much advantage has error in this reſpect, that let two perſons with equal powers of oratory ſet out; the one, to teach our holy religion in all it's purity; the other, to propagate ſome wild enthuſiaſtic notions about it; the number of converts, I would venture to ſay, made by the former, would bear no proportion to thoſe of the latter.

would fuit but ill with the grace and dignity of the matron. It is for this reafon, that all our poets apoftatize from their religion, and turn worfhippers of *Apollo* and the Mufes ; and, when they want any ftrong coloring, are obliged to have recourfe to *Pagan* rites and ceremonies: fo that, if by any means the *Pantheon* fhould be loft, one half of them would not be intelligible to the *Englifh* reader. Even the great *Milton* himfelf, is but a kind of heathen-chriftian, having plainly fhaped his angels after the pattern of *Homer*'s deities. How much it is for the honor of our holy religion, to have it's facred myfteries dreffed in the garb of heathen mythology, fhall be left to others to determine.

Thefe things being confidered, whether we may pretend to rival the ancients in point of eloquence, I know not. Having had little accefs to the houfes of parliament (the only places, I fufpect, where any thing like true oratory is practifed among us) I have never heard our Englifh *Demofthenes*; from fome * fpeeches however, occafionally

pub-

---

* It would certainly do our countr' no fmall credit, if a collection of fome of the beft fpeeches in parliament was feparately publifhed, *Debates, Journals*, &c. being too voluminous to find them in.

publifhed, one would be inclined to think, if we fall fhort of the antient orators in any thing,

The Clergy muft excufe me for not mentioning the Pulpit on this occafion ; as I am fatisfied, there is not much eloquence fhewn there; though more now, than formerly has been.

Indeed it is not eafy to determine, how much it ought to be practifed there. From the fpecimens of what one fees *Whitfield*, and his crew, able to do with mankind, by a very coarfe application of this talent, one might conclude, it would not be much for the quiet of the community, to have the paffions much ftirred by religious eloquence. And this is the mif-fortune of all eloquence, that it's greateft influence is over the weakeft underftandings, where it is juft as likely to do harm, as good. All therefore, which probably ought to be attempted from the pulpit in this way, is manly fenfe and fober reafon, with a very moderate proportion of ornament, and a ferious, earneft, emphatic elocution. But this is humbly fub-mitted to the judgement of the great *National Preacher*, who knows fo much better, what his in-brethren ought to do.

As for the Bar, the practice and method of plead-ing there, affords the modern advocate little oppor-tunity of difplaying any thing like eloquence. Our laws are fo numerous, and adjudged cafes fo com-mon, that the pleader has little elfe to do but to explain their intent and meaning, on the one fide ; and on the other, to puzzle and perplex it : as for any addrefs to the paffions of the judge or jury, cafes of doing that, with any propriety, feldom hap-pen, except in the occafional trials of ftate criminals; in which inftances our lawyers have always done juftice to their character, and their clients.

thing, it can only be in action; (which however, it muſt be owned, was adjudged to be
almoſt the whole of the matter by one of
it's greateſt maſters, though his opinion does
not give one the higheſt idea of it's worth)
as for ſenſe and language, theſe ſpecimens
are clearly equal, if not ſuperior, to any
productions of antiquity.

But let not the choir of *Parnaſſus* be a-
larmed : notwithſtanding the uncertainty,
which I have expreſſed about eloquence ; I
do not mean ſo tamely to give up the bays.
On the contrary, could my vote determine
it ; I would give it in favor of the moderns,
without heſitation.

With regard to language, after all the
pains, which the *Greeks* and *Romans* have
taken with their's ; they are both as far
from being philoſophic languages, as our's,
or the *French*; and contain almoſt as many
anomalies in them: in point of perſpicuity,
the advantage, by means of particles and
auxiliaries, ſeems clearly on our ſide: and
for numbers, all antiquity cannot produce
ſuch an inſtance of their power and harmony, as *Dryden*'s Ode on Saint *Cecilia*'s Day.

But the cauſe of the Muſes is of too much
conſequence to be reſted on one ſingle in-

ſtance,

ſtance, however ſtriking it may appear, And yet to enumerate in a particular compariſon all the Odes, Elegies, Epics, &c. which ancient and modern wit has produced, would be an endleſs buſineſs, in all ſenſes. Perhaps we may ſhorten the inquiry, by dividing poetry into three diſtinct ſorts, as it is more immediately directed either to the head, the heart, or the imagination. The firſt kind is that which has been called the *didactic*; the ſecond will include the *elegiac* and *dramatic*; and under the * third, may be ranked the
loftier

---

* I have reckoned that ſort laſt, which, I know, is by thoſe of high taſte eſteemed the firſt ; but when the poet neither inſtructs me, nor raiſes in my breaſt any tender emotions, he ſinks, in my eſtimation, into a character, very little ſuperior to that of a wire-dancer. I may ſay with *Horace*,

'   Ille *per extentum funem mihi poſſe videtur*
    Ire poeta*.

But then all he does, is merely to ſurpriſe me with inſtances of art and agility. He may indeed ſometimes, by the pictures which he draws, or the harmony of his numbers, riſe to the praiſe of a good painter, or a ſkillful muſician. But at beſt, I ſhould as ſoon compare *Giardini*'s tricks upon the fiddle to ſound muſic; as the ſublime *Epic*, or ſtar-ſtriking *Pindaric*, to the more chaſtiſed kinds of poetry; where the muſe condeſcends to be the handmaid of philoſophy ; and endeavors to give her miſtreſs freſh charms, whilſt ſhe is employed in delivering the great precepts of truth ; in tracing out the ſpring of
human

loftier fort of *Odes*, together with the defcrip-
tive, that is, far the greateft part of the *Epic.*
Every

human actions; in laying open the fources of our
paffions; and teaching us, how to moderate them.
The great Thunderer's nod, in *Homer*, has no charms
for me; indeed the only line almoft, which I ever
read in him with fincere pleafure, is that, in which
the penfive, unhappy father is defcribed, after his
fuit had been rejected;·

" Βη δ' ακεων παρα θινα πολυφλοισβοιο θαλασσης."

Though perhaps there may be fome reafon to fufpect, that the pathos even of this line is more accidental, than defigned. The circumftances, which
give the heightening to it feem to be principally the
place, where the old man takes his walk; (the fea-
fide being peculiarly adapted to melancholy con-
templation;) and the contraft between his grief-bred
filence, and the noife of the beating furge, ftrongly
conveyed to the mind by the epithet, πολυφλοισβοιο.
But as for his walking by the fea-fide, there was probably nothing more intended by it, than merely to
fignify his going out of the camp, which was fitu-
ated juft by. To fhew, that the poet did not choofe
this piece of fcenery, as peculiarly fuited to his purpofe on this occafion, we may obferve, that he makes
the *Greeks* do almoft every thing there — παρα θινα,
or επι ρη[μινι θαλασσης, they eat, fight, and play. And
as for any peculiar beauty in the epithet, πολυφλοισβοιο, his ufing it always indifcriminately, whenever
the metre requires fuch a word, inclines one to
think, that it owes the propriety, which it has in
this place, more to our ideas, than to his; who feems
to have meant nothing more by it, than he does by
his επεα πτεροεντα; νηα μελαινην; or indeed almoft a-
ny other of his epithets; which appear, in general,

.10

Every other ſpecies, of whatever denomination, is but a different mixture of the above.

To

to be choſe more on account of their being dactyles
or ſpondees, than for any other aſſignable reaſon
whatever. Why elſe do we hear of ποδας ωκυς Αχιλ-
λευς, or κορυθαιολ☉ Εκτωρ, when the buſineſs is only
to make a ſpeech? where υποδρα ιδων, or χωομεν☉ κηρ
might have a propriety, but the others none. Thus
we have πολυμητις Οδυσσευς, when his honorable em-
ployment is no more, than what the greateſt ideot
might have performed, as well as himſelf; only to
take thoſe by the heel, whom *Diomede* had knocked
down, and drag them out of his way,

——————— Αταρ ΠΟΛΥΜΗΤΙΣ Οδυσσευς,

'Οντινα Τυδειδης αορι πληξειε παραςας,

Τον δ' Οδυσευς μετοπιθε λαβων ποδος εξερυσασκε. Il. X.

He might have found a much better opportunity,
for uſing this epithet a little below (had not he been
guided in his choice by the reaſon above mentioned) where *Ulyſſes*, by a moſt ſurpriſing ſtretch of
thought, diſcovers that his bow will ſupply the place
of a whip; but here he uſes a very different one,

Τοφρα δ' αρ' ὁ ΤΛΗΜΩΝ Οδυσευς λυε μωνυχας ιππυς,

Συν δ' ηειρεν ιμασι, κỳ εξηλαυνεν ομιλυ

ΤΟΞΩι ΕΠΙΠΛΗΣΣΩΝ, επει υ μαςιγα φαεινην

Ποικιλυ εκ διφροιο νοησατο χερσιν ελεθαι.

Ροιζησεν δ' αρα · &c. ——— ΚΟΠΤΕ δ' Οδυσσευς

ΤΟΞΩι · τοι δ' επειολο, &c.   Il. X. ỳ. 498.

What is here ſaid of *Homer*, and elſewhere of
other ancients, is not meant, ſo much, to point
out any defect in them; (whoſe merit, all things
conſidered, muſt be acknowledged to be very great)
as to ſhew the want of candor in critics, who
weigh their merit, and that of the moderns, in very
different ſcales; and will not throw in the ſame
grains of allowance in the one caſe, as in the other.

To give an inftance of comparifon then in each of the three forts, can it be at all doubted, but that *Pope's* Ethic Epiftles far excel every thing of the kind in ancient poetry? Will not *Milton* be allowed to ftand at leaft, upon the fame level with *Homer* and *Virgil?* And may not fome Odes, lately publifhed from *Strawberry* Hill, juftly claim the precedence of any in *Pindar?* The fecond fort then is the only one left, in which the excellence can be difputed with us. And even in this, with regard to the *elegiac*, one need not be afraid of meeting with much contradiction, if one fhould fay, that no age or country ever produced an elegy, comparable to that in a *Country Church Yard.*

But in point of dramatic perfection, it feems on all hands agreed, that the moderns muft give way to the ancients. If we afk, why? it will be anfwered, Becaufe we have no chorus in our plays; which however, it muft be owned, got it's place in thofe of the ancients more through neceffity, than choice. It had the right of prior poffeffion, which could not eafily be fet afide. Plays at firft, were nothing but little interludes, made to diverfify certain choral fongs, in honor of *Bacchus,* the firft fpecies of the drama, that
ap-

appeared. When thefe were improved into more regular and perfect pieces, the chorus ftill maintained it's place by virtue of it's age, and the deference, which was paid to it on that account.

That it adds a dignity to the drama, muft perhaps be allowed; and to thofe, who are fond of fhows and proceffions, it would no doubt greatly enhance the merit of a play. That it is the guardian, or rather parent of the unities, is another point, which cannot well be difputed: for as it confifts of a number of perfons, got together in a great meafure by accident, it cannot well be fuppofed, that thefe can be kept together long; or be eafily removed from place to place. But then how confined, in refpect to variety, muft this needs render the drama? for how few actions, or plots are there of any importance, which will admit the fuppofition of being compleated in two, or even in twelve hours, or in one and the fame place? and if you once begin the magic of fcene-fhifting, it may as well be extended from the palace to the forum, as from one room in the palace to another.

They too, who judge from nature, and not from rules laid down by *Ariftotle*, and

a

a set of critics, whose aim it has been to follow him, rather than nature, will not perhaps be inclined to think, that probability is
much consulted by the introduction of a
chorus. An *acting audience*, which seems to
be the true character of the chorus, may, in
itself, be no very improbable thing: but an
acting audience, which at the same time sup-
poses another, *hearing*, audience present,
whose judgement it is to inform and regu-
late, is an utter outrage against all probability. Besides this acting audience, which is
to direct the other's judgement, (of the propriety and good tendency of which, to the
manners of the common people, a great deal
has been said) is generally so mysterious in
delivering it's own, that it is usually the
most difficult part of the play to be under-
stood: the songs of the Sybils themselves
could scarcely be more obscure, than some
of the *Greek* choruses must needs have been
to common understandings.*

 It is still more absurd to suppose, that a
set of persons fitted for the purpose, should
all

---

* What *Horace* says,

 Sortilegis non discrepuit sententia Delphis,
is true of the chorus in more senses, than one.

all be got together, without any apparent or previous reaſon for it, prepared with the fineſt flights of poetry; ſuch, as do not ſeem to ſpring from any ſentiments of the heart, excited by the turns and incidents of what is tranſacting, but are merely the viſionary work of imagination, carried into too long a train of diſtant ideas to ariſe from any preſent, momentary impulſe: and theſe, to take the buſineſs ſtill farther out of nature's path, are to be accompanied by the higheſt ſtrains of harmony, and all the pomp of muſic.

That they too, who conſtitute the chorus, ſhould either follow the principal character into his private apartment, where he might properly deliberate; or that he ſhould deliberate aloud in an open court-yard, before fifty different perſons; who are all to be made acquainted with the inmoſt * ſecrets of his heart; and yet are to interfere no otherwiſe, than by advice; when perhaps the very worſt of actions and deſigns are carrying on; are all of them matters, which accord but ill with the common notions of what conſtitutes the probable.

Laſtly,

* *Ille tegat commiſſa,* — and that of all the characters indiſcriminately.

Laftly, that a fet of inferior characters, (fuch as the chorus in moft cafes muft confift of, that the upper parts may be filled with proper dignity) fhould have influence to controul; authority to dictate; or underftanding to advife, and to deliver the great precepts of truth; is fuch a ftretch to all feeming, as nothing, but the poet's licence, *quidlibet audendi*, can poffibly give a fanction to.*

Many

---

* For an inftance of the impropriety, intended to be marked here, let any one read the ΤΡΑΧΙΝΙΑΙ of *Sophocles*; in which the chorus, who ought to read lectures to *Hercules* " de dolore tolerando," confifts of nothing better, than merely a fet of goffips : call them prieiteffes, or what you will, an old woman can be nothing, but an old woman : and a young one cannot well be fuppofed to have much influence, in matters of morality.

` `Accordingly, after*Hercules* appears upon the ftage, this refpectable chorus, of young or old ladies, whichever they be, does nothing like what *Horace* determines to be it's duty —

(*Ut regat iratos, et amet pacare tumentes*)

offers not a word, either to comfort *Hercules*, or vindicate *Deianira*; but immediately, as if confcious of it's own infignificance, feems to fhrink away to one fide of the ftage, and ftands almoft mute for the remainder of the play ; only the leading lady juft informs us, that " Her hair ftood on end at hearing " of her mafter's misfortunes :" that " It muft be a " fad thing for *Greece* to be deprived of fuch a " man:" and that " She was determined to ftay to the " end

Many other particulars might however
have been taken notice of; ſuch as, one
perſon's expreſſing the ſentiments of twelve,
or any number of others, without any mutual conſultation; which is the caſe of the
acting part of the chorus; or, a number of
perſons delivering the ſame ſentiments in
preciſely the ſame words, which is the caſe
in the *ſinging* part. The circumſtance of an
OMNES,

" end of theſe diſmal doings, (perhaps, to ſee the
" funeral) though to be ſure, nothing of this ſort
" could happen, without *Jupiter*'s having a hand in
" it." Theſe are the only obſervations, ſhe has to make
upon the occaſion, which, as *Shakeſpear* expreſſes it,
ſeems to be " The true butter-woman's rate to
" market." Though it muſt be owned, the monſter-
killer lets himſelf down as much, as he well can, to
their level, by the moſt feminine complaints, that
ever an opera-hero uttered : for a ſpecimen, hear
him,

　　Αι Αι ω ταλας, ϊ, ϊ.

This makes a whole line in a long ſpeech of his,
conſiſting of 130; that is, if the common diviſion
be right, within five lines as long, as the whole Third
Act; very natural, no doubt, for one in his circumſtances, dying, as he deſcribes himſelf to be,
with excruciating pains ! — Where too could an
Engliſh tranſlator find whimpering interjections,
enough to render this puny lamentation by, unleſs
he went to miſs in the nurſery, juſt as little maſter
had bit her finger, or ſcratched her doll's cap off ?

　I ſhall ſay nothing of the little attention, which
ſeems to be paid to the article of time in this play, not-
with-

OMNES, in one of our plays, agreeing in the fame form of expreffion, has frequently afforded matter of juft ridicule to the critics; how much more juftly might this fame circumftance have provoked their cenfure in the chorus, where it is carried to a much greater height of abfurdity? Such a parcel of lifelefs mutes too upon the ftage, (which could be but ill avoided by making a firft and fecond chorus) muft hang like fo

many

withftanding it is wrote in *Greek*, and has a chorus; though to preferve any thing like a unity in this refpect, *Hercules*, *Hyllus*, and *Lychas*, muft all be fuppofed to have travelled in *feven-league boots*. Neither fhall I take notice of many other ftrange particulars, fuch as *Hercules*'s defiring his fon to marry his whore, who had been the caufe of his mother's death; &c. becaufe they are not much to the prefent purpofe.

It might however be difficult for any one to affign a good reafon, why *Hercules* is brought upon the ftage at all, unlefs it were merely to fhew, how loud he could roar; as he never makes his appearance, till the fifth act; till the principal character is dead, and the chorus has fung her laft fong; that is in fhort, till the play, or at leaft all the diftrefs of it, is over. But perhaps the poet knew he could not raife in his audience an idea, of diftrefs enough, on *Deianira*'s account, nor even on *Hercules*'s, unlefs he exhibited him ALIVE, and made him bellow a little : as if the *Athenian* theatre had cried out, with the humorous Old Knight, " Prick me BULL-CALF till he roar : " but, could this be contrived for an audience of tafte ?

many dead weights upon every movement; especially in the *Greek* theatre, where, by being masked, they could not even shew the concern they had, in what was going on, by their looks and features.

Perhaps, if we must have a chorus, the only way of remedying all these inconveniencies, would be to form it of certain *Genii,* *Sylphs,* or *Gnomes,* — who might easily be supposed to be perfectly acquainted with all human transactions, without having any right to interfere in them; and yet might take a pleasure in hymning their sentiments about them. The songs of these imaginary beings, might give as many breathing times to the poet and his audience, as he thought proper; (for it is not easy to see the necessity of their being precisely five, though both *Greek* and *Latin* authority has determined it so) And being intirely under his management, he might take care to let them sing only just so much, as would be to his purpose,

— *Quod proposito conducat, & hæreat aptè.*

These songs would undoubtedly fill up the space, between the Acts, with much greater dignity, and propriety, than the poor shifts of a ballad, or a dance, which at present we have recourse to. Here too would
be

be room for. all the powers of mufic to fhew themfelves.. And here the poet might be properly delivered of all the towering flights of imagination, which could not be fo fitly introduced into the more fober drama. Into thefe characters, befides, he might throw as much oracular wifdom, and moral inftruction, as he pleafed: whilft, in the mean time, the acting part of the chorus, in the body of the play, might be much more naturally fupplied, as it is amongft the moderns, by a friend, or a confident.

It may be objected to this, that it would be likely to encourage fuperftition among the vulgar ; but what is there fo perfect, as that no objections can be made to it?

In fhort, as the great bufinefs of the ftage is, to pleafe us into inftruction and improvement; to humanize the heart, either by deceiving it into temporary pleafure, or by affecting it with imaginary ills, and fancied fcenes of diftrefs ; the poet, who has the greateft power over the imagination; who can, for a certain time, carry us with him, in his fancy's chariot, wherever he lifteth ; provided he does not hurt or fhock * us

by

* By *us* I mean thofe who are guided by their natural feelings, not thofe, who are governed by a

G   capri-

by the violence of his motions, ſeems to purſue the beſt and moſt probable path for obtaining his end. In this light all the ſons of *Apollo*, ancient and modern, do not equal the ſingle worth of *Shakeſpear*; *Shakeſpear*, " whoſe eye (to uſe his own beſt words)

——— " *In a fine fancy rolling,*
Doth glance from heaven to earth, from earth to heaven; &c.

And who (as he elſewhere expreſſes himſelf) " Holds as it were the mirrour up to " nature; ſhews virtue her own feature; " ſcorn her own image; and the very age and " body of the time, his form and preſſure."

However, if the old method muſt needs be thought the beſt; there is an inſtance ready at hand to ſhew, that the moderns can excel the ancients, even in their own way. It will eaſily be gueſſed, I mean *Caractacus*; which, for the auguſt and ſolemn ſcenery, the majeſty of the characters, the dignity, propriety, and poetry of the chorus, exceeds the moſt perfect model, which the ancients have left us.

I

capricious and whimſical taſte of their own acquiring; whoſe greateſt *pleaſure* conſiſts in being as much *diſpleaſed*, as poſſible; and who therefore ſeek for as many opportunities of being ſhocked, as they can find.

I have been carried fo far in the road of criticifm, that I am led to fay fomewhat of the thing itfelf.

How much beyond former clumfinefs then, are the modern refinements of this art? how elegant, delicate, and correct, are the Notes and Comments, lately publifhed on Two Epiftles of *Horace?* and what a mere *Florilegium* does even *Longinus* appear to be, when compared with the philology, contained in the *Ideas of the Sublime and Beautiful?* In fhort to fuch a pitch of improvement has this art been brought; that one may venture to affirm, there is more good fenfe and rational criticifm, to be met with in one of our common * *Monthly Reviews,* than in all the old *fcholia* put together.

But to fay the truth, Critics and Commentators ufually infeft only the lighter, and more trifling parts of fcience; fuch as poetry, philology, &c. juft as wafps and hornets fettle about hollow trees, and unfound earth:

---

* Perhaps this will be looked upon, as a *fop for Cerberus :* I cannot fay, that was my original intention in making the comparifon; but if it anfwers that good end, and carries me fafely paft that frightful monfter, I fhall have the higheft opinion of my own good management.

earth : and there is, for that reaſon, this plain ſign of ſuperior ſtrength and ſoundneſs in modern learning, that this ſort of infects dare ſcarce attempt to faſten upon it. There will never be the ſame number of critics and commentators, upon *Locke* and *Montesquieu*, that there has been upon *Plato* and *Ariſtotle*. And why? becauſe the opinions of the latter are ſo vague and undetermined, that they afford ample room for conjectures and explanations; whereas the former are ſo accurate and precise, any attempt to explain them would but render them confuſed. It is from hence poſſibly the complaint has ariſen, which one has ſometimes heard made by thoſe, who have had the education of youth committed to them, that they found it extremely difficult to read lectures, at leaſt to their own ſatisfaction, upon *Locke*. The caſe really is, he has left extremely little for any one to add to what he himſelf has ſaid.

CHAP.

C H A P. VIII.

Some general obfervations on ancient and modern learning.

TO clofe this long difquifition about antient and modern learning, the different lights, in which they may fairly be confidered, feem to be as follows.

The view of antient learning, where every now and then a ftriking fentiment appears, is not unlike that of a wide extenfive country, uncultivated for the moft part; but in which, here and there, you will difcover a pile of magnificence; which, from the fitua-tion it is in, receives an additional grandeur. Whereas the modern ftate of fcience refem-bles more fome favorite fpot of ground; on which every thing, that either labor or art could contribute, has been freely beftowed; where the whole is in a manner finifhed and complete; but, for want of contraft, no parti-cular part is fo likely to catch the attention.

It is from hence, that the ancients are thought to abound more in the fublime, than the moderns. Barren countries always afford the moft ftriking profpects : the ΔΕΙ-ΝΟΝ and the ΦΟΒΕΡΟΝ are moft remark-able there.

It

It is for the ſame reaſon ſome have imagined, they excel us alſo in *Genius*. Having
had the firſt free range into nature, they ſeized
to themſelves, what they eſteemed moſt worthy of their regard; juſt as the firſt travell-
ers in an unknown country mark down the
moſt remarkable mountains, lakes and rivers,
which they meet with there. But then they,
who come after them, and take a more accurate ſurvey, cannot juſtly be ſaid to have
leſs genius, than the others, or to be only
their imitators; though perhaps they give us
the ſame rivers, lakes, and mountains, which
the others had done before.

. The moderns too, by their practice of
quotation, have greatly contributed to leſſen
their own character in this reſpect, and to
raiſe that of the antients. At the revival of
learning, all the knowledge in the world
was neceſſarily drawn from the old foun-
tains, which were now again laid open; and
men were ſcholars in proportion, as they were
more or leſs acquainted with theſe. Afterwards, when they began to think a little for
themſelves; as if they had been afraid to go
alone, or truſt themſelves out of leading-
ſtrings, they were glad to ſeek for ſupports,
to what they advanced, in the opinions of
the

the antients; which by this means were raifed to fuch a degree of authority and importance, that what was matter of choice in a great meafure at firft, became in time almoft neceffary; fcarce any thing being thought right, which was not confirmed by fome inftance of former wifdom to the fame purpofe. Men, for this reafon, were put upon ftraining the fentiments of the ancients to meanings, which they never dreamt of: and from hence, in many cafes, the moderns have been fufpected of borrowing from them, what in fact they firft gave them, by their own forced interpretations.

It is no concern of mine however, to decide the controverfy of merit between the two. All I am inquiring about is, only, to find out, who know the moft; not what merit each might have in acquiring the knowledge, they are mafters of. *Columbus* might have more merit, as the Difcoverer of *America*, than *Hernan Cortez* had; — but, notwithftanding his pretenfions, it is certain, the other penetrated farther into it; and may, without any injury done to the former's reputation, be ftyled, and have the praife of being, it's Conqueror.

CHAP.

CHAP. IX.

Of the art of War.

THE art of war is ſo totally changed, that it is hardly poſſible to compare, what it is with what it was.*

However, if it is become rather a more ci-vilized buſineſs; if the work of bloodſhed be ſooner over; if the fate of a pitched battle be ſooner decided; if the carnage, which enſues, be leſs dreadful; and the conquered, eſpe-cially that unfortunate part of them, who are made priſoners, be treated with greater †humanity; we may well ſay, it is improv-ed. We might alſo appeal to living inſtances of Heroes, greater than any, which *Rome* or *Greece* ever ſaw; whoſe fame was chiefly owing to their having to deal only with barbarous

and

---

* " If in any thing we deviate from the practice " of the antients, it is in our military diſcipline, in " which we are ſo abſolutely new, that there is ſcarce " any thing uſed, that was preferred by our an-" ceſtors." *Machiavel.*

† The ſubſcription now going forward in favor of the *French* priſoners, wretches left to ſtarve by their own king and country; will be a laſting honor to this nation in point of humanity! but this conſide-tion properly belongs to another place.

and unpolifhed nations; whom it was fcarce any merit to conquer, their own unfkilful-nefs had fo great a fhare in the victor's fuccefs.

But, however true it may be, that the world is improved in this, as well as in'other inftances; how much more defireable a truth would it be, to fay, that our other im-provements had rendered all attention to this lefs neceffary !

And did not the matter of fact, of almoft all *Europe*'s being engaged in war at prefent, ftand in our way; it might perhaps be no difficult undertaking to make this appear a probable hypothefis. One may fee, how, by the firft inftitution of government, private quarrels were, in a great meafure, fuperfeded; the feuds and animofities of particulars be-ing made fubject to the decifion of common laws. The imperfect ftate indeed of thefe governments at firft left room, too frequent-ly, for particulars to difpute the public au-thority: and hence arofe the calamity of ci-vil war. But now, by the improvements made in moft of the governments in *Europe*, we have ceafed in a great meafure to hear that worft of founds, the din of civil dif-cord. May there not then be fome room to
hope,

hope, from theſe two ·gradual advances towards perfection; that, if *Germany* and ſome
of the other leſs perfect ſtates here, with the
whole unſettled Weſtern world, (which have
of late afforded the chief materials for public broils) were to receive the ſame improvements, which other ſtates have; there would
almoſt an end be put to all occaſion for
public, as well as civil wars? when we
ſhould ſee the law of nations have as full
effect, as the law of particular kingdoms:
when that moſt deſireable of all prophecies,
yet unfulfilled, might receive it's full com-
pletion; when, " Nation ſhould no more lift
" up ſword againſt nation; neither ſhould
" they learn war any more."

   If there be not room to hope for this,
there is at leaſt ſufficient reaſon to wiſh for
it; ſince what deforms the fair and regular
appearance of things ſo much, as the horrid
outrages of war; even when it is conducted
by the beſt rules, which civilized nations
have impoſed upon it, to tame it's fiercer
ſpirit?

   However, till this moſt happy event can
take place, we may well add the following
wiſh to the former;—that ſo long, as war is
to be the reſource of empires, quarrelling with
                                                each

each other, *Britain* may never want fuch
* gallant hearts and able heads, to defend
her interefts, as have lately raifed her glory,
and their own honor to fuch an amazing
height !

✝ As the Soldier's character, fo long as it is neceffary, muft ever be one of the moft refpectable
in all ftates ; and may well claim every inftance of
praife from us fons of peace, who enjoy the eafe,
which they, at the hazard of their lives, purchafe
for us ; fo fhould nothing prevent me from offering
the poor tribute of my praife, on this occafion to all
thofe, who have, during the courfe of this war,
done fo much honor to themfelves and their country ; but that their number renders a particular
mention of their names almoft impoffible : fince if
I once began to quote the particular perfons, who
deferved to be diftinguifhed, I fhould almoft write
a complete lift of his Majefty's forces, both by fea
and land, from the Admiral and General, down to
the common feaman and foldier ; and fo fhould make
it no diftinction at all : indeed there can not well
be any made, but between thofe, who have been
in fervice, and thofe, who have not ; which laft, if
they had had the fame opportunity, would, I am
perfuaded, have difcharged their duty as faithfully,
as the others.

CHAP.

CHAP. X.
Of Religion, conſidered as a Science.

AS to Religion, men ſeem to have fol-
lowed their ſenſes firſt, in the choice
of objects to worſhip; their paſſions, next;
and laſt of all, their reaſon.

Even the Deity, in the different revelations of himſelf to mankind, ſeems to have
acted in a manner, ſomewhat analogous to
this.

To our firſt father and early patriarchs he
appeared in bodily ſhape, like a man; the
higheſt degree of excellence, to which their
ideas probably then reached. He afterwards
cloathed himſelf in more majeſty and ſplendor; and was not viſible to the *Jews*, but in
clouds, or in fire: ſtill however did he talk
even to them of the ſtrength of his arm, and
the furiouſneſs of his wrath; and endeavoured to influence them to a diſcharge of
their duty, by ſetting before them temporal
rewards and puniſhments; the weakneſs of
their underſtanding, even yet, not ſuffering
them to look at any higher things. But at
laſt, when the fullneſs of time was come, he
" brought life and immortality to light;" and

has

has reprefented himfelf, as far as it was poffible, to our narrow comprehenfions, as he
is ; in doing which he feemingly confidered
mankind as having now attained to ftronger
powers of reafoning, and therefore capable
of receiving more fublime truths, than heretofore ; " the Law having been ftrictly," as
the fcripture fays, " our SCHOOLMASTER
" to bring us unto *Chrift*." *

How-

* Perhaps a reafon, as fatisfactory as any other,
might be deduced from hence, why Chriftianity has
not been more extenfively difperfed in the world,
than it is. A great part of mankind may be, for
ought we know, really incapable, through their ignorance, of receiving it.

But then to folve, how this itfelf fhould come to
pafs, would be another inquiry, as difficult as the
former ; in the purfuit of which, if any one fhould
fay, " that mankind appeared to confift of feveral
different fpecies, naturally diftinct from each other,"
what great degree of abfurdity would there be in
the fuppofition? We fee this, in fact, is the cafe, with
regard to Dogs, and fome other Kinds of animals ;
among which one fpecies fhall greatly excel another, both in beauty, fagacity, and, if I may fo fay,
even in good manners. Why therefore may not the
fame obtain amongft Men ? appearances are certainly for it : or why, otherwife, fhould the *Hottentots*
and wild *Indians* have continued, from the firft date
of their exiftence to the prefent period, with fo few
marks of improvement amongft them ? It is not e-
nough to fay, that they fhew themfelves capable of
learning things from us ; (for fome even of the inferior

However, to speak ingenuously, it is rather our happiness, than it ought to be our
pride,

ferior animals are capable of that, as far as their or-
ganization will allow them) but the question is, if
they really have the same power of perfecting themselves; or, to use a new word, if they are indued with
the same perfectionability, which we are; why have
they not struck out of their own accord new disco-
veries; and advanced in improvement, as we have
done?

It might be objected to this way of reasoning,
that it seems to preclude the Christian Religion
from ever attaining to that universality, which both
from it's own nature, and from some not obscure
prophecies, it was apparently designed to have.
Now this objection would be removed by supposing
that *our* species, which for distinction's sake may be
called the *European*, shall in time possess the whole
earth, to the intire exclusion of all the rest. And, if
we may guess at consequences, from what has happened within these last two centuries, this will not
appear a very absurd hypothesis. Neither is any
great violence done to truth by supposing, that some
species of beings, even of mankind, may become ex-
tinct. What is said both in Scripture and Pagan
accounts, about Giants, makes it not improbable,
that this has already been the case : and it is evident, that the number of wild beasts is greatly dimi-
nished ; some whole kinds, such as *Wolves*, which
appear to have been formerly the most numerous,
scarce existing now, but in pictures and relations ;
and for specimens of others, we must send much farther, than heretofore was necessary.

It may be observed, as a consequence from hence,
that if the slave-trade is to be defended at all, it must
seemingly be on some such principles, as the above.

pride, that we excel former times in this article. It was the wifdom of God, and not of men, which brought this to pafs: we ought therefore to give God the praife. And yet, oddly as it may found, it is not abfurd in fact to fuppofe, that even a religion given by God himfelf, (perfect as it muft have come from it's all-wife Author,) may receive, reference being had only to the minds of men, many new additions of beauty and excellence, by being better underftood.*

I would not here be thought, to caft the leaft reflection on the primitive affertors of gofpel truth. But furely they had better hearts, than heads. And one would rather praife them for their honeft and upright intentions, than condemn in any refpect men, to whom we owe fo much. Without cafting any blame upon them, it muft be owned, that learning was declining apace; when Chriftianity was left to human means for it's fupport. It was not long afterwards, that

---

* Nothing feems clearer, than that many things even in this laft revelation, were delivered in the manner they are, merely in compliance to the weaknefs of their ideas, to whom it was firft made; which would have put on a very different appearance, had knowledge been in the fame ftate of perfection then, which it is now.

that our Religion, with almoſt every thing elſe, was buried in the ruins of the *Roman* empire; where it lay hid in darkneſs for ages.

Whoever conſiders this, and reflects farther, how lately it has emerged from this obſcurity; how ſtill more lately it has been able to diſentangle itſelf, in any degree, from that ruſt and rubbiſh, from thoſe great errors and groſs ſuperſtitions, which it had contracted in thoſe dark cells, where it had been ſhut up; and which by length of time, were grown ſo cloſe to it, that they ſeemed, and were long * thought to make a part of the Religion itſelf ; whoever, I ſay, conſiders theſe things, will not be ſurpriſed, either that Chriſtianity has not hitherto been better underſtood ; or, that it is better underſtood now, than ever it was, ſince inſpirati-

on

---

* It was indeed no eaſy taſk to ſeparate the two, or to point out diſtinctly, where true and genuine Religion began, and where theſe ugly, adſcititious envelopments ended. Perhaps to ſome it may ſeem, as if a part of theſe ſtill hung round it, which a too great tenderneſs may have hitherto ſpared, left by taking off a wen of a confirmed growth, the health of the body itſelf ſhould be endangered. And certainly, if ever this ſhould be attempted, the greateſt ſkill and care will be neceſſary, to prevent all ill conſequences.

on ceafed; now, when men's underftandings are more refined, and their refearches into truth more enlarged, than ever they were before!

There are not wanting however fome amongft us, who are for fhortening thefe refearches; and tell us, it is enough without any thing farther, if we only know, that fuch a thing *is written :* in which opinion, it may be worth while to obferve, they feem to differ a good deal from St. *Philip* ; who, upon feeing a perfon with a Bible in his hand, was not content with merely afking him, what he faw written there; but made this farther inquiry, " Underftandeft thou " what thou readeft ?" And how this bufinefs of *underftanding* is to be accomplifhed, without the act of reafoning, without inquiring, by whom any thing was written; on what occafion; with what probable defign; how it agrees with other parts of Scripture ; and poffibly alfo, how confonant it is to our own notions of God, and the relation we ftand in to him; is, I own, a point, far above my comprehenfion.

One would not fuppofe, that thefe men thought the Scripture falfe; but furely they talk, as if they did: for what harm can in-

H quiries

quiries about it do, if it be true ? it is the nature of all truth to love the light; of error, to avoid it. The one acquires fresh charms by being more clearly seen; and the uglinefs of the other can no otherwife be fully detected, than by being brought into public view.

They would do well too to tell us, before they take the ufe of our reafon away, what difference there is, between a falfe Religion, and a true one falfely underftood. Let them go to the banks of the *Nile*, and there find out the diftinct worth of the *Copti*, and his neighbour the *Muffulman*.*

Or if they do not like to go fo far abroad for inftances, let them look into fome of our modern affemblies of the faithful at home, and point out to us, the fpecific difference of enthufiafm and fuperftition, when built upon Chriftianity, and the fame, when arifing out of any other mode of worfhip.

---

* See an account of the old Serpent, and many other curious Anecdotes about them, in *Norden's* Travels, Vol. 2.

CON-

CONCLUSION.

IF the above confiderations are fo fortunate, as to evince the point, for which
they were thrown together; and fhould
make it feem probable, that there has been
almoft a continual improvement in human
Knowledge; they may poffibly at the fame
time fuggeft a fufpicion, that we ourfelves,
whatever high attainments we may boaft,
fhall be far outdone by thofe, who come after. But let not this damp our eagernefs to
get as near perfection, as we can; let it rather animate us, with frefh zeal, to leave as
few things unfinifhed, for pofterity to excel
us in, as may be.

The End of the Second Part.

ERRATA.

Page x. *of the* APOLOGY, *&c. line the laſt; for* their, *read* it's.

Page xi. D°. *line the* 7*th; after* "don't, *dele the* comma, *or the word* "act.

Page viii. *of the* EXPLANATION, *&c. line laſt but one; for* " or leaſt, *read* "or at leaſt.

Page 84. *in the Note, line* 22 ; *for* " in-, *read* inferior.

Page 99. *line the* 10*th; for* philology, *read* philoſophy.

www.ingramcontent.com/pod-product-compliance
Lightning Source LLC
Chambersburg PA
CBHW020013030726
47500CB00002B/575